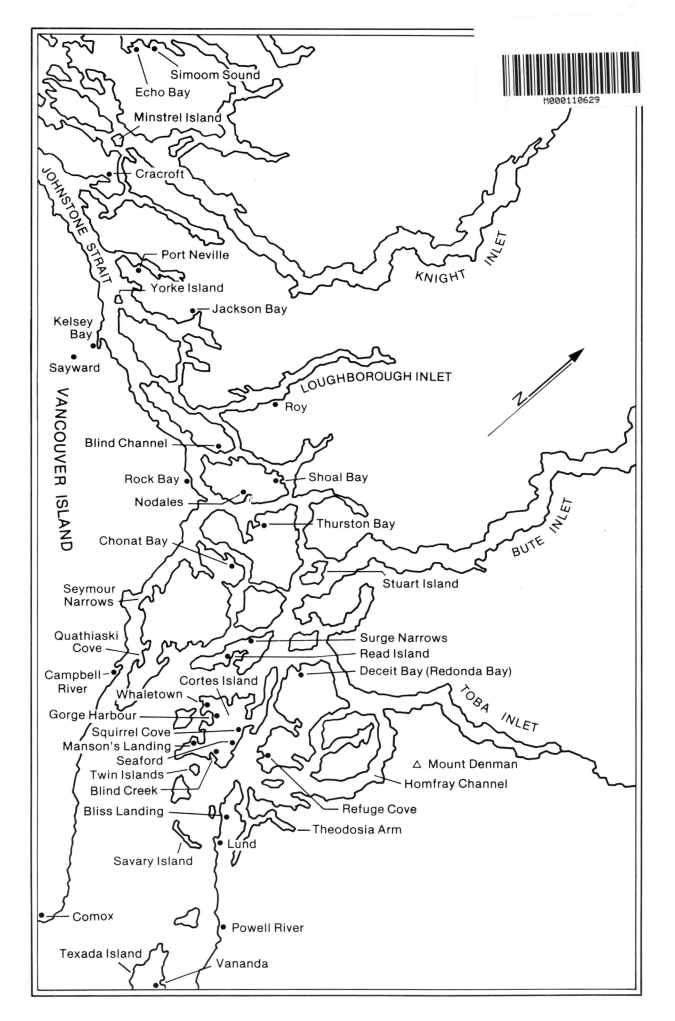

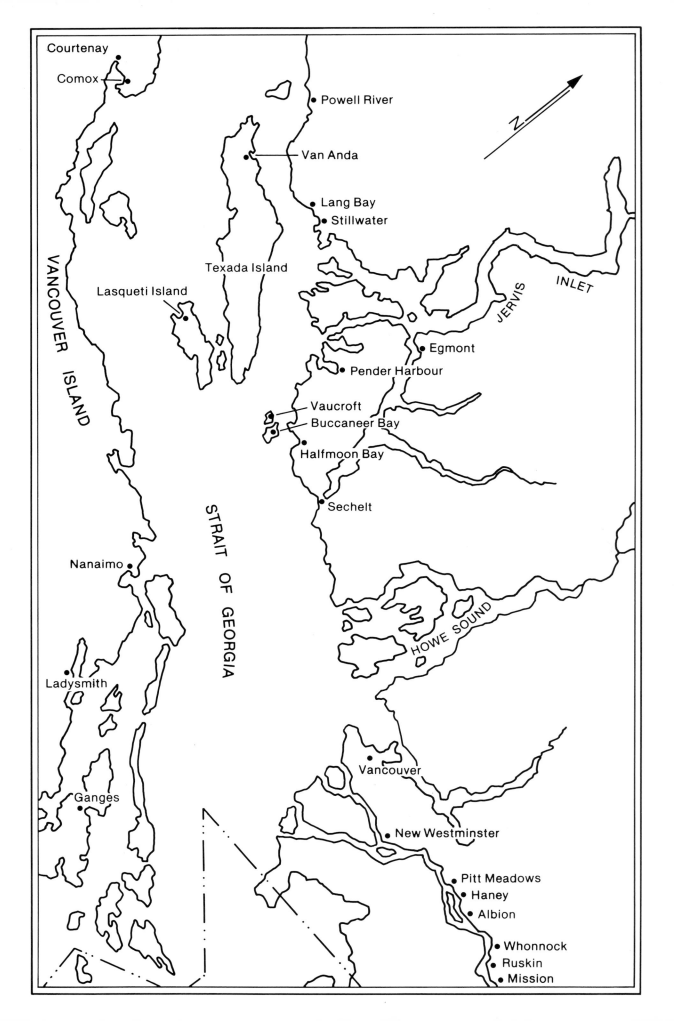

SPILSBURY'S ALBUM

SPILSBURY'S ALBUM

**Photographs and Reminiscences
of the BC Coast**

JIM SPILSBURY

Harbour Publishing

First trade paperback printing 1995

Harbour Publishing
P.O. Box 219
Madeira Park, BC Canada V0N 2H0

Edited by Daniel Francis
Cover art by A.J. Spilsbury
Cover design by Roger Handling
Design by Fiona MacGregor
Printed and bound in Canada by Friesen Printers

Published with the assistance of the Canada Council and the Government of British
   Columbia, Cultural Services Branch

Canadian Cataloguing in Publication Data

Spilsbury, Jim, 1905–
   Spilsbury's album

   ISBN 1-55017-126-7
   1. Frontier and pioneer life—British Columbia—Pictorial works.
2. Spilsbury, Jim, 1905–   3. British Columbia—History—20th
century—Pictorial works.   I. Title.

FC3817.3.S65 1990   971.1'0022'2   C90-091598-6
F1087.S65 1990

Contents

Introduction

With the appearance of my first two memoirs about life on the BC coast, *Spilsbury's Coast* and *The Accidental Airline*, I realized that some people got as big a kick out of the photographs that went along with the stories as they did from the stories themselves. Any irritation the storyteller in me might have felt at being upstaged by mere pictures was relieved by the fact the photographs were from my own collection and were largely my own work. In fact there were hundreds more I hadn't been able to fit into the books and it wasn't long before I found myself talking to my publisher about a third book that would make use of a larger pictorial format to give the photograph collection the kind of prominence it seemed to crave. A game sort, he agreed to give it a whirl, but a curious thing happened along the way. While I was looking over all these old photos trying to come up with concise, pithy captions, I accidentally wrote 35,000 words of new stories. Some of it grew out of the pictures but some of it had a life distinctly its own.

The book still follows the haphazard method of the family album and the photographs still provide the backbone. Taken up and down the coast between the First World War and just yesterday, they record the great changes which have taken place on the coast since I first came here as a child. I suppose that many of the scenes I was lucky enough to witness may never have been photographed by anybody else.

To a large extent, I wouldn't have trusted my memory alone to tell many of the stories in this book or the two previous ones. They seem so improbable sometimes. I'd think, "Well, I must have been dreaming." But then I'd have these photographs, and I knew that I wasn't dreaming. It *did* happen, and I *was* there.

I suppose you could say that photography is in my blood. I didn't realize it at the time, but some of my earliest memories are of photographs. From a young age, I was surrounded by people who were accomplished photographers, and this must have had a lasting influence on me.

Childhood recollections are sometimes partial and distorted, crowded out by more recent happenings. But I can remember quite clearly many of my family's traditions. In particular, I recall the overpowering importance attached to the past: the family in England with its ten generations of history; the stained-glass windows in the church that read SPILSBURY; the cemetery full of family gravestones, which my old Aunt

Bella decorated with fresh flowers all her life. No one seemed to talk about the future. Was there going to be any?

Feeling so strongly the weight of the past, I suppose it was only natural for me to look around for something less depressing, more interesting. I discovered the present! I could do something about that. I was so pleased with my discovery that I developed the urge to record it for others to enjoy, and at first I tried to set it down in drawings and paintings. As business involvements made my time increasingly precious, I turned to photography as the ideal medium.

I was certainly not the first photographer in my family. In the 1890s, my Aunt Bella took up photography as a hobby. She took all kinds of pictures of me as a baby in England, and when my parents came back to British Columbia the family gave Dad a camera with instructions to take lots of pictures of me. The camera was a folding Brownie. It had a bellows, and used Kodak 116 film which was smaller than postcard size.

Dad used that camera for many years, and he certainly got darn good pictures with it. He used what in those days was called "Soleo" film; he would dip it in a solution, then develop it in the sun.

My mother's friend, Ethel Burpee, also took excellent photos, some of which I have reproduced in this book. I was five or six years old when I first remember her taking pictures, and she definitely spurred my interest in photography.

In 1922, when I went to work at a shingle bolt camp up Homfray Channel, Dad loaned me his old folding Brownie, and that is when I started taking pictures myself. I didn't take very many in those days, mind you, because of the high cost of film. The original lens of the Brownie was very simple, but I replaced it with an F 7.5 anastigmatic lens. Everyone was talking about the anastigmatic in those days, and I got pretty good results with it for several years. Then I left it on the beach one time and the tide came in and that was the end of that.

Shortly after, Dad's dear old friend Harry Hall gave me all his photographic equipment. It included an Aldis Butcher, quarter plate reflex camera, with an F 4.5 lens. I think it was Harry Hall more than anybody else who explained to me the principles of photography. This camera took excellent pictures. I lugged it all over the coast, even packed it up mountains, complete with glass slides, cut film adapters and a large, wooden tripod.

I'd been used to mailing my film to Dunn and Rundle in Vancouver

Candid cameraman.

for developing. But Harry also gave me all his developing equipment. This was about 1929 or 1930. I built an enlarger, using the bellows and lens from a defunct camera. I developed and enlarged my own pictures for several years.

During the 1930s, the Vancouver Art School used to run an off-season camp on Savary Island, my home for many years. Twenty or thirty students used to stay at the Royal Savary Hotel, and, as part of my taxi business, I carted them around with all their equipment. One day I was taking some photographs of these students when one of the teachers, an old fellow with a pointed white beard, happened along. He was Mortimer Lamb—a Vancouver art critic, a supporter of the Group of Seven, and a very high-brow, avant-garde photographer, at least so I was told. He kindly took me under his wing for an hour or so and gave me instruction concerning the artistic point of view. He had me photographing stepped-on crab shells, dead tree branches, and all kinds of strange stuff I never would have given a second thought. I couldn't see what he was aiming at. I was more interested in making a record of what I saw, taking pictures to show people where I'd been. When I saw something new, or different, the first thing I would think was gee, I better get a picture of that.

What I didn't realize until years after was that my mental camera was working along on the same principle, snapping memories of novel and curious events and people which would come back to me in words. The great discovery of my later years has been that so many things which caught my eye along the long and meandering path which has been my life also strike a spark of interest in others. I hope readers of my third book will find this continues to be true.

I took my camera with me everywhere, even to the tops of mountains.

CHAPTER ONE
Savary Island

Savary Island became my home in 1914, when I was nine years old. This was where I grew up, went to school, worked with my dad, learned to use tools, learned to hunt and fish, had my introduction to logging. In the process I met and got to know the motley collection of people who inhabited the coast in those days, ranging all the way from loggers, fishermen, and beachcombers to hermits, remittance men, stump ranchers, Greek scholars, writers, poets, artists, and downright crooks. It was a community of people that surely was unique in the history of man, and I had the good fortune to spend the next thirty years of my life with them.

Going back a ways, my grandfather was the Church of England clergyman for the parish of Findern in Derbyshire, as were his father and his father's father before him. My own father was the youngest in a family of five boys and four girls. Aside from going away to college or private school, they all stayed home and enjoyed life as ''landed gentry'' supported by ''The Governor,'' my grandfather, and the income he derived from the tenant farmers in the parish.

In other words, they did nothing—useful, that is! Until something got into my Uncle Frank, the eldest son. In 1878 he took off for the colonies, first by steamer to New York, then across the United States by the Southern Pacific Railroad to San Francisco, then by paddle-wheel steamer up to New Westminster where he hired an Indian to paddle him up the Fraser River to find a spot to camp. He found one that appealed to him near Whonnock, where he bought a couple of quarter-sections. He shacked up with an Indian mistress and spent a few years hunting and fishing, always with lots of hired Indian help. Eventually, though, he grew tired of this life and persuaded his younger brother, my Uncle Ben, to buy him out. Uncle Frank returned to England where he settled in with another mistress and concentrated on doing nothing, to a good old age.

Then it was Uncle Ben's turn to get a taste of life in the backwoods. He liked it less than Uncle Frank, and it wasn't long before he wrote back to England and persuaded another younger brother to buy *him* out.

This was my dad, who at that time was in his second year at Cambridge studying medicine. Uncle Ben's description of the wild frontier, and the hunting and fishing, appealed to Dad, so in 1889 he took his inheritance money, came to BC, and bought out Uncle Ben. He was only eighteen years old.

Dad spent many years and all his money turning that land into an ideal farm. He cleared forty acres, ditched and drained it, and had twenty acres under intense cultivation, including a fair-sized fruit orchard. He borrowed $20,000 from the Westminster Trust Company and built two silos, the first in the Valley, quite an innovation. He shipped fruit and vegetables to the market in New Westminster, and milk and cream twice a day on the ''milk train.'' He always hoped to make money, but never did.

My dad met my mother, Alice Maud Blizard, when she came out from England to spend the summer with her brother, who had a stump-ranch in Fort Langley. They were married in Vancouver in 1898. A former housekeeper of Dad's, who had met and married Charlie Thulin, the founder of Lund, wrote to Dad telling him what a wonderful place it was, and all the country around there, so he and my mother decided to go there for their honeymoon.

They travelled up by steamer and booked in at the hotel. In those days there was no Powell River, and aside from the mining town of Vananda, Lund was it—the end of the road. In a rented fourteen-foot, double-ended rowboat they started out to explore the country thereabouts. They rowed over to Savary and spent the first night in an abandoned log cabin, the only building then on the island. It had been empty since the owner, Jack Green, was murdered two years earlier.

They stayed several days on Savary, where Mother shot a deer and they caught some salmon and ''planked'' it Indian-style. Then they casually rowed across the Strait of Georgia to Oyster River where they camped for several days. Mother shot a bear and a cougar, the smelly hides of which graced a couple of chairs in the living room for years to come. As a kid I was always afraid of them in the dark! This ''voyage

My grandmother and my grandfather, the Reverend B.W. Spilsbury, in about 1870, not long before their son Frank, the eldest of my uncles, came out from England and established the Spilsbury clan in British Columbia.

of discovery'' made a lasting impression on them, and they decided that if and when they sold the farm they would build a comfortable ''motor boat'' and spend their time cruising the coast in style.

In 1905, when it became apparent that I would arrive, my father's family insisted that my parents return to England for the occasion. No way would they approve of my being born in the colonies! Elaborate arrangements were made to get people in to operate the farm in their absence, and two weeks later, by train and steamer, they arrived in England. And that is how I came to be born October 8, 1905, in the same upstairs bedroom where Dad was born. So I was born an Englishman, something I've been trying to live down ever since!

During this stay in England, Dad contracted rheumatic fever. He spent the better part of six months in bed under the care of the family doctor, who solemnly declared that Dad would never again be able to do any physical work. To make matters worse, members of the family made it very clear that they did not approve of my mother's social status. Her father was in the garment trade in London, and quite well off, but as far as the Spilsburys were concerned, he was ''in trade.'' They considered Mother a caste below them and they didn't try to conceal their contempt. She never got over the experience—her whole life changed. From then on she made Dad's life miserable, and later, mine. She refused to wear ''female'' clothes. She wore men's pants, she cut her hair short like a man's, she got involved with the suffragette movement. She was one of the original women's libbers. She attracted a lot of attention and a lot of people admired her, thought she was ahead of her time. But she took it all out on Dad and me, and life was not very pleasant for us.

When we got back to Whonnock, Dad got busy salvaging what was left of the farm. The people had not looked after it and the place had deteriorated. In spite of the doctor's warning, Dad was soon working harder than he ever had in his life trying to get the place back in shape, with the hope of eventually selling it. He did sell it, in 1912, to a local farmer. The substantial down payment enabled him to build a new house on some spare property and then make a down payment to the shipyard for the boat and engine he had planned for.

My parents decided to take a well-earned holiday at Lund, about 150 kilometres up the coast from Vancouver. At the old hotel where we were staying, we met Colonel Lawrence Herchmer and his wife and daughter. The colonel took us over to see the cottage he was having built on Savary, and he offered to let us live there for a winter. I was seven years old, and it was my first visit to Savary Island.

And then came the First World War. The people who had bought my parents' farm took advantage of a wartime moratorium and stopped making payments. But Dad had to go on paying land taxes, and this was more than he could afford since he now had no income of any kind. In the end he lost everything, boat, engine, farm. Dad was the only Spilsbury of that generation who really did any work and he was the only one who ended up without any money.

Meantime, he was desperate for a way to keep a roof over our heads. It was at this point that he and Mother decided to take up Colonel Herchmer's offer to live in his cabin on Savary for the winter. Dad could do some work building fences for the colonel and I could go to the new school that was just opening on the island. In the fall of 1914, we made a temporary move to Savary—and we stayed for thirty years.

At the end of the first year, it came time to move out of Herchmer's cabin. Without money to go anywhere else, we simply set up our tent and squatted on an unused road right-of-way just west of the island wharf. We squatted there in varying degrees of poverty for ten years. Then, in 1924, my grandmother died and Dad got the last of his inheritance money. This enabled us to buy some property and build a house, which still stands at the end of the government wharf.

When we arrived on Savary, there were maybe thirty or forty permanent residents, and the school had fourteen students, spread over five grades. I was almost nine and I had never been to school before,

but my father had taught me to read and write, to do some arithmetic, even algebra and a little trigonometry. I went to school for four years and as far as I can tell I learned nothing that I did not already know. I was always getting into trouble and those were undoubtedly the four most miserable years of my life. When I graduated from grade eight, the nearest high school was in Powell River. There was no way the family could afford to move, so that was the end of my formal education.

After I finished school, the plan was for me to go to sea. It was 1919, and there was no way I could get into the Canadian Navy, but Mother managed with the help of an influential friend to get me into the merchant marine. I was taken on as an apprentice by the Canadian Robert Dollar Steamship Company and was assigned to the good ship *Melville Dollar*. I lasted five months, for one trip across the Pacific to China, Japan, and the Philippines. I was seasick and homesick the whole time. On my return to Vancouver I stepped ashore for good, disillusioned but wiser.

In a funny way, though, my stint at sea did end up steering me into a career. On board the *Melville Dollar* strict discipline prevented me from speaking to any of my superior officers. All the rest of the crew—64 in all—were Chinese who couldn't speak any English. However, on occasion and without the captain's knowledge, the wireless operator let me in his cabin to watch him operate the big ¼-KW spark transmitter. I was fascinated and I became determined that when I got ashore I would get enough money to buy the parts to build a receiver of my own. I would listen to the ships talking in Morse code and practise until I got my code speed up. Then I would go to Sprott-Shaw School and get my ticket to be a ship's wireless operator.

But how to make some money?

It so happened that a small logging show turned up on Savary about then and started to log some timber at the place we called the Springs. I and the two Tait boys got jobs—this was the beginning of my logging experience. I was hired as a "knotter" and "swamper" for a flat 25 cents an hour, eight hours a day, six days

My three aunts: l. to r.: Kate, Bella, and Bess. Bella was a fine photographer, who indirectly got me started with a camera.

a week. We sometimes waited several weeks before we got our money. Then I got work in another camp up Theodosia Arm, and after about two years I worked my way up the scale until I ran a steam logging donkey and got seven dollars for a nine-hour day.

While I was in camp I bought the materials and assembled a "crystal set" that would receive Morse code and later on—music. Finally, when I had a thousand dollars saved, I quit the logging camp and went back to Savary. I gave half the money to Dad so he could finish building the house, and I used the other half to buy radio parts. Customers were coming to me now to get their radios repaired, or to buy new ones. I put up a large painted sign on a tree in the Ragged Islands (Thulin Pass)—"Radio Expert, Savary Island." Tugs and fish boats would come over to get their sets fixed. Business kept growing, and I never looked back.

A family group, c. 1907. Seated, l. to r.: Aunt Kate, Uncles Frank and George, my grandmother and grandfather, Aunt Bess. Standing, l. to r.: Uncles Humphrey, Ben, and August. This is when Aunt Bess took Uncle August back to England to present him to the family. He was part Indian, from Albion in the Fraser Valley. Aunt Bess married him to spite her brothers, then legally changed their name from Baker to Boulanger as a bit of snobbery. They lived at Whonnock until World War Two.

The Longlands, in Findern, Derbyshire, home to many generations of Spilsburys. This photograph was taken about 1905, the year I was born there in one of the upstairs rooms on the left. That's my grandfather, the "Governor," in the doorway to the greenhouse. The place looked much the same when I saw it again during a visit to England in 1951.

My father, Ashton
Wilmot Spilsbury,
about the time he
married my mother in
1898.

That's me, about three years old, at the old farmhouse in Whonnock, built by Uncle Ben and my dad. Down on the left were two grass tennis courts and in front was the croquet lawn. There are some necessities that English people could not do without!

This picture of me was taken by my dad with the camera the family in England gave him to keep track of my growing up. I'm helping Uncle August saw timbers.

Previous page: The CPR stern wheeler *Beaver*, leaving our farm at Whonnock. This was the most convenient transportation to New Westminster.

A view of the lower part of the farm, c. 1906, looking across to the river. The cabin near the riverbank was built by Uncle Frank in 1878.

Getting my sea legs in my first boat, a converted horses' drinking trough.

My first pair of skis, on the hill behind the farm.

This is the house, under construction, that we built at Whonnock after Dad sold the farm to finance his dream of cruising the coast in a boat.

We lived in the second house for about a year before we moved to Savary Island.

My first girlfriend, Laurencia
Herchmer. She later married
Hugh Rickard and still lives on
Savary Island.

That's my dad rowing the Herchmers' boat, c. 1914. I am in the bow keeping watch; Mrs. Herchmer and Laurencia are in the stern.

This is The Front at Savary, before anybody much lived there. That's our tent on the left. We lived in it from 1914 until 1924. In the centre is the first actual house on the island, built by Louis Anderson. Louis was a timber cruiser who settled on the island when he married Irene Palmer of the famous logging family. The house still stands. We kept our boat in the structure on the right.

Home sweet home. This picture was taken shortly after we moved in, when the tent still had a canvas roof. Before too long it rotted and was replaced with a split cedar roof. The sides of the tent rotted as well, and finally there was very little left of the original canvas.

A closeup of Louis Anderson's house, with our tent in the background, c. 1916. The road that now runs the length of the island started up the hill right over top of where our tent used to be.

My bedroom in the tent. All Mod. Cons.! Note brush, comb and lamp.

FISHING

When my dad first came from England to take over the farm at Whonnock, he was very short of money. He decided to earn a little extra income in the summer by going gill-net fishing in the Fraser River. He got a job with Neil Cameron, a dour old Scotsman with only one eye. Cameron had an overgrown rowboat with a mast, a lug sail and a pair of oars. It was Dad's job to row the boat; I think they called him a "puller." Cameron lived in Ewan's Slough in the Fraser just below New Westminster.

At that time the government only allowed fishing six days of the week. A cannon was fired on Sunday afternoon as a signal to start fishing for the next six days. The fishermen would set their nets to drift in the main river or sometimes off the mouth. During the six-day week, they never came ashore, just slept on the boat. There was no means of cooking, so they had cold food, usually salt salmon and pilot biscuits. At night, if it was raining, they pulled the sail over the mast or the oars to make a little shelter.

Sockeye was very plentiful. Dad said that sometimes they would only get half their net out before it got so loaded with fish that they'd have to bring it back in. Sometimes there were more fish than the boat could hold and they had to throw the excess overboard.

The cannery paid seven cents for each sockeye salmon. Since the supply usually exceeded the demand, to be fair they only bought a limited number from each boat. The rest went overboard. Nowadays, fishermen are getting $20 or more per fish!

There were problems. Some of the paddle-wheel steamers didn't bother to go around the fishermen's nets. When the fishermen saw one of these vessels coming up the river, they would have to haul in the nets as fast as they could.

There were hundreds of men with similar boats fishing for salmon in the Fraser and in the other rivers up the coast. Dad thought the whole thing was ridiculous because there were such things as permanent fish traps. A trap consisted of rows of pilings with nets to guide the fish in through a narrow opening and collect them in a pond. Then all the men had to do was bail them out of the pond into a scow and take them to the cannery. Indians had used this method for centuries. Three or four men could get more salmon into the cannery than a hundred fish boats. But the government banned traps. They were too efficient; they did not produce enough jobs.

Dad said that occasionally they would catch a sturgeon. Some of these fish were enormous, several hundred pounds. When they got one, they didn't sell it because there was no market. But it was good for food, so they would put a rope through the gills and tie it up to the riverbank. Every time they needed a meal, they would go down and chop steaks off it, starting from the tail and working up. The sturgeon was good for two or three weeks, tied to a stump and swimming around on the end of the line. Most of the farmers along the river kept sturgeon this way.

When we moved to Savary Island, fish remained an important part of our diet. We depended on it, in fact. We caught salmon when they were available and salted them down for the winter. It was really quite a simple process. In those days, the Japanese imported pickles from Japan and threw the empty casks away. These five-gallon pickle tubs, to be found on the beach, were just the right size for salting salmon. First you laid about four inches of coarse salt in the bottom of the tub. Then you threw in a layer of fish fillets and covered that with salt and continued layer after layer until the tub was full. Then you put a flat stone, about fifteen or twenty pounds, on top of the salmon to press it down. The salt gradually dissolved and the liquid had to be poured off and more salt added several times, but after that it kept indefinitely.

There were quite a few commercial fishermen working out of Lund. They all had small boats, about thirty feet long with probably one-cylinder, 4-5 horsepower gas engines. They were slow and had minimal accommodations. In season, the men trolled for salmon; at other times the boats were re-equipped to jig for ling cod.

In the centre portion of the hull, each boat had what was known as a "live-box." There were two watertight bulkheads about ten feet apart with limber holes cut in the sides of the boat so that this compartment was always full of clean salt water. This is where they threw their catch of ling cod as they caught them, keeping them there until they had a load to sell to the buyer. Cod lived several weeks in the live-box. At that time there was no market for red snapper, but the average boat caught three or four red snappers for every ling cod. The fishermen simply threw them overboard as they caught them. Red snapper usually come up from very deep water, and as they approach the surface they cannot stand the decompression. Their stomachs come out of their mouths and choke them. I can recall seeing long strings of these bloated red fish floating away from the stern of every codfishing boat—miles of them.

On the island our method of fishing was very simple. We had to row our boat by hand. We used a heavy, green cotton fishing line with a fairly heavy weight attached, and a steel wire leader with a spoon on the end, usually a "Stewart." It was a wobbler about four or five inches long. We didn't just go down to a sporting goods store and buy these things ready made. We went to the store in Lund that served commercial fishermen and bought pieces of sheet brass. Some were plain brass, some were nickel-plated. With a pair of snips, we cut the brass into suitable sizes to make a spoon. Then, with a ballpeen hammer and a block of wood, we made each end concave. This is what made it wobble in the water. If I was fishing by myself, I rowed just fast enough to keep the spoon wobbling and my fishing line was tied around my foot so that I knew if I got a strike. Mother was different. She insisted on using a fishing rod and reel. She didn't catch any more fish, but I guess she had more fun.

My dad on his way to the smokehouse.

Mother and Dad with a day's catch, standing in the beach grass that grows all along the shoreline on Savary.

Planking salmon the Indian way at Indian Point. It's still the best way to cook them.

My mother dressing a salmon on the shore.

Mother on the left, and Ethel Burpee. An excellent photographer, Miss Burpee took most of these early pictures of Savary.

A memorable day fishing. Mother hooked a fourteen-pound Spring salmon, which was promptly swallowed by a forty-one-pound ling cod and the two fish were landed together. The story made the Vancouver newspapers.

Miss Burpee sitting on a boat she rented in Lund. It was in a boat exactly like this one that my parents spent their honeymoon touring the coast.

The Union Steamship boat *Cheakamus* arriving at the Savary Island wharf on one of its twice-weekly visits. That's me on the left, peeking around behind my mother.

WATER ON SAVARY

I doubt that anyone can tell us for sure just who dug the first well on Savary, and where. Some would say that it must have been old Jack Green, who had the first log cabin at the east end of the island well before the turn of the century. I clearly remember his well, just behind the cabin, about twelve feet deep and lined with split cedar planks. Eventually it became dangerous and we had to fill it in for safety reasons. But was it the first?

I have my own theory. Heavy clamshell deposits are ample evidence of Indian habitation at the east end of the island, from the point to the wharf. Indians only camped where there was fresh water, and the closest spring was four miles away. I bet they dug a well just about where old man Green's was. Digging was comparatively easy in the loose gravel, and in the back part they would have had to go down ten feet or less. There is no other explanation for the heaps of clamshells.

In 1911-1912, dozens of lots were sold, summer cottages were built, and the original Savary Inn was erected—all the doings of the Savary Island Syndicate. Harry Keefer was the moving spirit, as well as the local postmaster, storekeeper, and manager of the inn. The Syndicate had its problems, one of which was the fresh water supply. Their modern-sounding solution was to dig a communal well, install a communal pipe, construct a communal reservoir, then pipe the water the length of the new townsite to every house.

The well was large, six feet square, with real wooden cribbing, and deep enough to have four feet of water in it. They installed a Fairbanks-Morse one-cylinder, double-action geared pump, driven by a Fairbanks-Morse one-cylinder vertical, 5 horsepower, "make and break" 4-cycle engine that ran on distillate. The very latest thing.

This was all housed in a locked building at the foot of the hill on Blair Road.

At the top of the hill, they constructed a large concrete reservoir, capable of holding over a thousand gallons of water. Louis Anderson is reputed to have packed every bag of cement up the hill on his back; there was no other way to get it there. A 1½-inch galvanized pipe ran from the pump up the hill to fill the reservoir, and a second pipe ran from the reservoir back down the hill to supply the townsite. From that point they installed a four-inch tarred wooden pipe all the way along the road to the far end of the settlement—over two thousand feet of the stuff buried in a ditch. This was supposed to supply the Savary Inn and the forty or so summer cottages. When the system was ready to turn on, Harry Keefer got the honour. (In his spare time, he was the engineer in charge.) He cranked the engine over and away she went. Water trickled out of the "up" pipe into the reservoir and it began to fill.

Everyone climbed up the hill to watch the water rise in the tank. It got to about eight inches deep, and then the water stopped coming. The well was dry! Trouble was, it took a day to fill again. So it took about a week and a half to fill the reservoir, even though they pumped twice a day. The well was in very fine sand. They couldn't have picked a worse place on the island to get water, but they needed a hill to put the reservoir on.

I don't think any cottages ever permanently hooked up to this system. In the summer of 1914, people filled buckets from places where the wooden pipe was leaking, and in one or two places faucets were installed. It soon became apparent that there was not enough water for everybody, so the pipeline was closed off and all available water went to the hotel.

After a year or so, the Syndicate sold the Savary Inn to Miss Ruth Roberts, who always wore a one-piece brown knitted dress, and her sister. They couldn't run the pump, so I got my first regular job. It was the only internal combustion engine on the island at that time, and I felt it gave me a great deal of prestige, as well as teaching me a good deal about internal combustion engines. Several years later, when Val Nichols bought the hotel and added cabins and more plumbing, the water supply could not cope. At my dad's suggestion, we dug a new well right alongside the hotel. It produced unlimited quantities of water, and an electric pump and pressure tank took over.

By this time, almost every cottage had its own well and hand pump—thanks to old Louis Anderson. He was, by his own admission, a talented water diviner. He used a forked green willow branch. He always drilled a small hole in the point of the V, put in a few drops of mercury, and drove a plug in the hole. Louis attributed his outstanding success to this device, and he wouldn't tell very many people his secret. He had a flat charge of $5 to find water, and his success rate was 100%.

For us permanent residents, digging wells was one way of earning badly needed money, along with cutting firewood and helping to build houses. After Louis Anderson left the island, my dad and I took over most of the well digging. Because we didn't use a divining rod, people were a bit leery at first. So we had to make a deal: no water, no pay. We never got stuck.

We developed our own water divining theory. To prove our suspicions, we ran levels and depth measurements on a good number of wells in different locations, and sure enough, water was *always* encountered either at mean sea level or very close to it. So it really didn't matter *where* you dug a well.

Jack Green's log cabin, the first building on Savary. Green was a transplanted Englishman who ran a store, sold liquor to anyone passing by, and grazed a few cattle. By the 1890s, he owned most of the island. He was murdered, and the story was that his treasure was buried somewhere around the cabin. No one ever found it, but we sure tried hard. Hugh Lynn was convicted of the crime, and hanged. About 1932 the derelict cabin was considered a hazard and it was burned down.

A picnic excursion down the sand cliffs to the beach on the south side of Savary. As kids, we were organized by Jesse Williams, an early cottager, to plant broom plants all along the cliffs. One year he brought up a bunch of broom seedlings and he gave us all sharp pointed sticks and a sack of broom and sent us out to plant in lines down the slopes. British admiralty charts showed "Remarkable white sand cliffs," since become completely green with our broom.

The Willows Hotel at Campbell River, c. 1914. The village was not yet built.

Lund at the time of World War One. The large, white building on the left is the store, and next to it is the Malaspina Hotel. That was the new hotel.

The old hotel is the large building on the right. It was later used as an annex to the other one, until it burned down about 1916.

Another view of Lund. The large building in the centre is the store, and the Malaspina Hotel is behind it to the left. The boat on the left is the *Empress of Lund*. It was available for charter. In fact, the first time I went to Savary was on the *Empress of Lund*. On the right is the steam tug, *Cypress Queen*.

Frank Turnbull commands the Savary Island "home guard" during World War One. I'm first in line, dagger tucked rakishly in my belt.

That's my dad in the middle, wearing the latest in men's swimwear, c. 1915. I am seated in front of him just to the right, beside my mother, also decked out to go swimming.

PRINCE

Harry Keefer, the storekeeper on Savary, owned an old white horse named Prince. With considerable disdain, my parents, who were the horsey type, called him a Cayuse, whatever that is. The poor old nag was never intended as a riding horse. From when he arrived in 1914, his job was to tow an old black cart, which Mr. Keefer loaded with groceries and freight, up from the wharf to the store on boat day. And he did the job just fine. When he wasn't in harness, Prince spent most of his time standing around munching and minding his own business. He munched anything and everything. When he smiled, his front teeth stuck out at a 45-degree angle, like he could chomp carrot tops through a picket fence with them.

One day Frankie Keefer, the storekeeper's daughter, told the teacher she was going to take Prince out on the meadows and ride bareback. *Bareback!* What could they possibly be thinking about? I had read all about Lady Godiva and the ruckus she stirred up. This was a show I could not afford to miss. I tried to get Bill Ashworth to join me in a snoop, but he showed no interest. I figured

maybe he was a bit immature for this sort of thing. When I mentioned it to Jimmy Anderson, however, I got his immediate attention. ''Frankie Keefer? Wow!'' He signed up right away. So that afternoon, with keen anticipation, Jimmy and I stationed ourselves behind some bushes where we would get a good view of the proceedings. What a disappointment was in store for us. There was Frankie, fully dressed, holding on to the hair on the back of Prince's neck, and the horse slowly walking along, munching everything in reach. So the term ''bareback'' refers to the horse, not the rider? I wonder if Bill Ashworth knew this all along.

A few years after Prince arrived, a vegetable man began coming in a small boat to sell produce. He owned a small farm down the coast near Sliammon and he found a ready market on Savary during the summer. His boat was noisy and very slow and by the time he got alongside the float, all the ladies would be down from their cottages to snap up the best buys. This made Mr. Keefer pretty unhappy since his store was loaded with week-old vegetables from Vancouver. In the long run, though, he got his revenge.

The vegetable man took a shine to Prince so Mr. Keefer sold him for a good price, complete with wagon, thereby getting back all the money the vegetable man had made out of Savary Island customers for the whole summer.

The new owner loaded Prince and the wagon onto a very rickety-looking raft and began towing it down the coast to his farm. We all watched. As the raft passed Green's Point and drew near the mainland, old Prince saw his chance. He jumped overboard and swam ashore. The vegetable man didn't notice until he got all the way down to his farm. Next day he was back up looking for him. With a good pair of binoculars we could see Prince climbing very slowly up the steep, rocky shore, munching with every step and looking very happy. But from his boat close to shore, the vegetable man couldn't see him. Each day Prince was a little higher, and all the rocks below him were cleaned of grass and daisies. As far as I know, the vegetable man never did catch him. But someone living up behind Lund, to his great surprise, found himself a horse, a *white* horse of all things.

Frankie Keefer riding Prince.

The first boat my dad built. We never got around to naming it, we just called it "Our Boat."

Like several others, we acquired this boat on our beachcombing expeditions. It was a punt that drifted up on the south shore of the island. We used it for a couple of years with the outboard motor on the back.

The *Mary Taylor* was an old sealing schooner, beached for a long time near Lund. At some time during the war it was wrecked by loggers working in the bay, which now carries the name Mary Taylor Bay.

This is the only time I ever used a "rag hanger" of any kind. It belonged to Miss Burpee and was called the *Ethel B*. That's Bill Hind holding the paddle.

THE SAGA OF G & K LOGGING

The outbreak of World War One created a lively demand for logs on the coast. George Ashworth, later the founder of the Royal Savary Hotel, had acquired a block of property on the island just west of Blair Road. The property had some trees on it. Trees make logs, logs make money. Not one to overlook an opportunity, Captain Ashworth realized he had the makings of a logging operation close at hand, including the personnel. Louis Anderson was a logger and knew how to go about it. Harry Keefer, the storekeeper, claimed to hold a valid steam engineer's ticket. Theoretically at least, he could run a donkey. Bill Mace was handy with tools, including an axe, and could learn how to fall trees. My dad had similar expertise and was used to hard work. All of them could use the money.

Apparently all that was lacking was a steam donkey. So the Captain went to Vancouver to get one. He had no more money than any of the rest of them, and I don't know how he swung it, but in no time at all a tug and scow arrived with a steam donkey on board. They all had to admit it was a little on the small side, more like what you would see on a steam pile-driver in those days, but with one main difference. It had a very weird-looking main drum. It was spool-shaped, like a yo-yo—small in the middle and tapering up at the ends. It had been used by the Greater Vancouver Waterworks to haul a dredge bucket across the First Narrows when they were laying the first water line to Capilano.

Louis Anderson looked at this thing, pushed his hat back, scratched his head, and said something unkind, partly in Swedish. The unflappable Captain simply said that was the best he could do without any money. They'd better make the best of it and would Keefer please get off his butt and drag it ashore. The tug and scow were costing money he didn't have.

Now came the test. Could old man Keefer really run the thing? He puffed out his chest and assured Louis that he would take over as soon as someone provided him with some water for the boiler and enough wood to build a fire in it. So Bill Mace set about running a pipeline to the nearest well, and Dad set about beachcombing and splitting about a cord of wood. In the meantime, Louis struggled with the coils of some rusty old cable to rig a block purchase from a tree on shore so the donkey could pull itself off as soon as Keefer got steam up.

After much puffing and snorting, and with great difficulty, the little donkey pulled itself ashore and up to the foot of the hill. It seemed to have an acute case of asthma. The engine had no power, and foam bubbled out of the exhaust instead of steam. The water they had pumped from the nearest well had so much salt in it that it threatened to blow the cylinder heads off. Eventually they had to blow all the water out of the boiler and lay a pipeline all the way from the well that supplied the Savary Inn.

There was another problem. The little donkey didn't have enough power to pull itself up to the top of the hill, in spite of all the luffs and blocks that Louis Anderson could devise. They had to grade a roadway slanting up the hill and put cross skids on it. Dad did most of that work himself. Then, under Louis's instructions, they built a magnificent logging chute from the beach to the top of the hill. It was over 200 feet long, supported on a cribwork of logs about twenty feet above ground in the centre span. It must have contained more good fir logs than they ever put in the water.

After many long weeks of work, the chute was finished, the road up the hill was built, and the little steam donkey moved into place to start logging. In those days this was known as "ground yarding." The log was simply pulled along the surface of the ground by sheer brute force, digging itself into the sandy ground and collecting all the limbs and branches along the way until the donkey couldn't pull any more and got stalled. This made Louis Anderson very mad, and he used language that none of us had ever heard before.

No one was prepared for the complete change in Louis wrought by his sudden elevation to the position of hooktender and woods boss of the G & K Logging Co., as the locals were now calling the outfit, though not when "George" and "Kate" Ashworth were listening! Louis's amazing transformation began just as soon as he put on his new pair of Leckie's Caulk Boots, bought for the occasion. (He was the only one with proper logging boots; no one else could afford them.) Normally very quiet, gentle and patient, he would suddenly use fluent and extremely bad language on the slightest provocation. His eyes glazed over and foam appeared at the corners of his mouth, causing him to spit tobacco juice between floods of obscenity, all of which added extra drama to the moment. He would throw his hat on the ground and jump up and down on it with his caulk boots while he said the most unkind things about the little donkey, which he claimed "couldn't pull a cork out of a whiskey bottle." Then he would switch to the subject of Harry Keefer, who was well out of earshot, referring in particular to the size of his belly and his ineptitude as a donkey puncher. There was certainly some substance to his complaints, but they didn't make the job any easier for the crew.

As kids, we used to run up the hill right after school to watch the fun, usually getting cursed and told to "Get the hell outta the way!" On one or two occasions we sneaked up during the long evenings after the crew had gone home and we had it all to ourselves. If there was still a little steam pressure in the boiler, Jimmy Anderson climbed up on the machine and ran the engine very carefully. He'd been a whistle punk in his uncle's camp during school holidays and knew what he was doing. We would hook the choker to an old slab of a log and haul it slowly out with the haulback, then back into the donkey again. Two or three would ride on it until there was no steam left. It was tremendous fun.

I don't remember how long they operated, or how much timber they put in the water, but it was not enough to pay wages. G & K Logging ground to a halt. The little donkey sat up there by itself for quite a time, getting rustier and rustier. Eventually, Sealskin Naughton, a well-known character on the coast, bought it. He really did wear an ankle-length brown sealskin coat and a fur hat, even though it was then summertime. He arrived with a scow and a tug, and an engineer. They threw a fire in the donkey and started to move it to the scow but the engineer saw right away that the engine had no power. He got out his tools and readjusted the valve settings. Took him all of half an hour and presto, she came to life. Practically leapt off the ground when he opened the throttle. I have often wondered if the logging operation might have turned out differently if this malfunction had been detected earlier. On the other hand, we would never have learned so many swear words.

These horses are skidding logs on Cortes Island.

Harry Keefer alongside the first motor vehicle on Savary, our Model T truck. I must have backed over a stump or something, and the front wheels collapsed. That's the store in the background.

Chief Julius and his wife, from Sliammon village, at Lund, c. 1914. Natives from Sliammon used to visit Savary with baskets and so on for sale.

Indian rock paintings in Homfray Channel. They used to be very distinct, but the last time I went in looking for them you could hardly see the figures. People used to say that these paintings marked good fishing spots. I recall that when I was working up there we always found that if we went right under these rocks and jigged, we could count on getting a ling cod in the first five minutes.

Left: An Indian village up Toba Inlet in 1932. The cabins are on floats, and could be gone tomorrow.

SAVARY ISLAND CUISINE

My mother could cook, but only when she felt like it, and the results were not always attractive as far as I was concerned. She would throw a whole chicken in the pot and boil it, beak and all. I would have to leave the table when I saw the thing. My parents also liked mutton, which Mother would boil. I can still see half an inch of white fat on the top of the saucepan. To this day I do not eat mutton. Ducks and geese were considered a great treat, but the wretched things were always hung by the neck in the outside cooler until their tails dropped off—a matter of several weeks. They were not considered edible until they reached this stage. It was the same treatment for venison, which we got quite a bit of, in and out of season. The haunches were hung up to age all winter. They would become coated with an outside layer of mold. The meat didn't actually go bad, but it got to taste pretty strong. Other meat, including beef, which my parents referred to as joints,

they would never eat when it was fresh. It always had to be aged, usually for several weeks.

Dad made porridge every morning. He always used stoneground oatmeal which would be soaked overnight in water, then cooked in the morning. We ate it with brown sugar and diluted canned milk. Dad was also the one who made bread. It was a two-day procedure. He used Royal Yeastcake soaked overnight to rise in the morning, and whole wheat flour or half and half. Mother occasionally made other things as a special treat—suet pudding, or gingerbread. For dessert, she often made rice pudding. She made it days ahead of time and kept it in the cooler. It had a skin on top like thin leather. After a while there would be mould underneath this skin, but you scraped it off and put on strawberry jam and that was dessert.

When all else failed, we fell back on Ramsay's Boston Pilot Bread, ''ship's biscuit,'' the same thing the British navy used for centuries. It was as hard

as plywood, impossible to bite through, but you could put one on a block of wood and split it with a double-bitted axe. Once you'd split it you had to turn it over and tap the weevils out.

There were many ways to use sea biscuit. For lunch, out on the job, we'd split them and spread them with peanut butter, and put a slice of cheddar cheese in the middle. Another treat was butter and a slab of Libby's corned beef. Sea biscuit was often used for breakfast. But for this you had to soak them overnight in water with a little Worcestershire sauce added, or maybe a teaspoon of mushroom ketchup. In the morning the biscuit was soft, and after you fried the bacon you threw the biscuit into the frying pan and fried both sides with generous amounts of black pepper. Biscuit also made an excellent dessert. We'd soak them in milk all day so they swelled up and got soft. On a saucer topped with strawberry jam? Delicious!

Mother always had chickens cackling around. This is their run behind our tent.

THE FINE ART OF DUCK HUNTING

People on Savary did a lot of hunting and fishing, just to keep food in the house. You pretty well had to make do with the weapons at hand. By the time I was nine I could handle a gun and contributed my share to the larder, mostly ducks of one kind or another.

One day I started out by myself to get a mallard. By this time I was allowed to use my mother's double-barrel 12-gauge shotgun. It was an Ithica with wire-twist barrels, one of the newer hammerless varieties. You cocked it by breaking the breach, then putting the button on safety until you were ready to fire. There were no mallard around our end of the island on this particular occasion, but a few had been spotted five miles away at Indian Point where they would be feeding in the seaweed.

As I crawled through the grass I sighted a group of about five birds feeding along the edge of the beach. By moving stealthily when their heads were down, I crawled away down behind a large log, which would put me about twenty-five feet from them when they reached that spot. Here I froze, and I do mean FROZE, for about two hours while the birds slowly worked their way towards me. I was peeking through some grass, and could see that they were getting very close. I was squatting, and had the gun muzzle just over the top of the log. With two barrels, I hoped to get all five of them.

I had received very strict training in the handling of a gun and was used to checking, and double checking, everything. At this point the gun should still be on "safe." I checked just to be sure, pulling back on the safety catch. To my horror, it moved back with a click. Did this mean that I had done the whole crawl with the gun in the firing position? If Dad found out, he'd kill me. However, the catch was back now, and just to make doubly sure I

pulled the trigger. BLAM! Both barrels went off. The butt kicked back into my thigh and gave me a beautiful purple bruise. The ducks all departed for Hernando Island. My ten-hour hike was for nothing. I think I cried all the way home.

Further investigation disclosed that the safety catch on the gun had not two, but three positions. After writing to the Ithica company about it, we learned that it worked as follows: Forward—Fire; Centre—Safe; Backward—Fire—*Hair Trigger*! My mother had used the gun for twenty-five years and never knew it. I got busy

Myself, with my trusty .22, returning from a duck-hunting expedition.

43

and put a large lump of solder behind the catch so it could not happen again.

Duck hunters traditionally use decoys, but as far as I can remember Savary had only one proponent of this method. This was Bob Townley. He enjoyed making things in his workshop behind the cow barn. He also shot ducks on occasion, contenting himself with the types that frequented the area near the wharf. In order to entice them closer, he made a flock of decoys that looked very much like the real thing. He used cedar floats from gill nets, painted them black with white patches, and attached carved heads. At first sight, they really looked like butterballs. He tethered them to the wharf where he could watch from the house. I'm not sure how successful they were in attracting ducks, but I do remember the time they caused a real flurry of excitement.

George MacFarlane was in his early teens. He had his father's shotgun, a belt full of cartridges, and a great yen to shoot something. Spotting the flock of decoys from a distance, he spent some time stalking them, finally opening up with a fusillade. He went through half his cartridge belt before getting wise. Bob Townley was not a bit amused. He had to make new heads for several of the decoys and did considerable grumbling about it. But that was not the end.

H.O. Wootten came up to the cottage a couple of days later and went out with his gun, a double-barrelled Greener, English-type scatter gun, to shoot at anything just for fun. He often had one or two of us kids go around with him to scare up the game—anything at all, ducks, crows, chipmunks. One of us had the bright idea of leading him down the beach to Townley's decoys. Well, what George MacFarlane hadn't quite accomplished, Mr. Wootten did. He just about demolished them.

This picture was taken for the family back in England, to show them how I was coming along.

Waves breaking on the beach at Savary.

MORE THAN ONE WAY TO TOP A TREE

The full donkey crew at the Palmer-Owen logging camp up Theodosia Arm in 1923 consisted of engineer (donkey puncher), fireman, wood splitter, and wood buck. I had come up through the ranks to fireman the previous year.

We had just moved the Empire steam donkey up the hill to its first "setting." This involved topping and rigging a spar tree 175 feet high. The regular high rigger wasn't there, so one of the owners, Bill Palmer, undertook to do it. Like all the others, he could climb, top and rig a spar tree when he had to. But this time, Bill was going to demonstrate a different method of taking the top off a tree. Instead of climbing up there with a six-foot crosscut saw and an axe, and spending an hour chopping and cutting, all he did was chop through the bark and make a notch around the tree. Then he got about twenty sticks of dynamite and wrapped them around the tree in the notch. On his way down the tree he lit a twenty-foot length of fuse, figuring this would give him enough time to reach the ground and get clear.

The fuse burned at three feet per minute, which only gave him about six and a half minutes. Partway down he started to get anxious and decided to speed up his descent by jumping down ten feet at a time. This is a trick that a high rigger will perform on occasion, just to show off. He throws about six feet of slack in his climbing rope, drops the loop down the back side of the tree as far as it will go, then jumps back away from the tree. Dropping about ten feet in a hurry, he jabs his spurs back in when he gets to the end of his rope. By repeating this process, a man can come down a 150-foot tree in less than a minute if everything works right. But this time it didn't.

Halfway down his jump, one of Bill's spurs caught in the bark or on a limb stub and he flipped completely upside down, landing with his back to the tree and his rope tight around behind him.

In this position, a climber is absolutely helpless. The only solution is for another man to climb up and rescue him. We carried a spare set of belt and spurs on each donkey for just such emergencies. But there was no time to do anything. The fuse was getting short. From a safe distance we all watched, and counted the seconds.

The noise of the explosion was deafening so high above the ground. Fragments of bark, branches and splintered wood flew in every direction. The entire treetop rose about a foot straight up before it fell over and dropped to the ground. When the smoke cleared, there was Bill, still hanging upside down about fifty feet below, mercifully unharmed and bellowing at us to "Hurry up and get me down!"

That's **Cliff Palmer**, being a bit of a show-off. The **A-frame** was erected on a large raft and the logs were yarded to it. The whole coast for 2000 feet back from the water was logged years ago using **A-frames.**

Left: **Bill Palmer's float camp in Theodosia Arm in 1923, when I was working in the logging camps.**

George Palmer starting up a tree.

George Palmer after topping a spar tree. Branches were left on the tree to prevent it from whipping violently when the top came off.

A steam locomotive on the logging railway operated by Merrill, Ring and Moore in Theodosia Arm. They had forty or fifty miles of track in there.

James Spilsbury, LDE (Logging Donkey Engineer), at the controls of an Empire steam donkey in Squirrel Cove on Cortes Island.

Raising a spar tree on the top of a hill.

Steam donkey at Squirrel Cove in 1924. On the left is the wood buck, sawing logs for firing the donkey. Then there's the wood splitter, who splits it up into chunks. The fireman is probably around back. And then there's myself at the controls running it.

Finally we are out of the tent. In 1924, after ten years of living under canvas on Savary, we built a house. And a fine house it was. This is the living room, looking into my bedroom which was also my radio room. That's the *Encyclopedia Britannica* by the chair. Dad wouldn't be without it.

Right: Our house from the outside.

Opposite: Our house just a year after it was built. We hadn't put the stucco on yet.

CHAPTER TWO

Radio Days

Broadcast radio came to Savary Island late one night in 1922.

In the years before the "radio," some of the summer kids I grew up with on the island used to invite me down to Vancouver during the winter. In their basements they were playing with radio, just as a hobby. It was all spark, of course. They had a spark gap about an inch long, a wire out into the cherry tree, a big smell of ozone, and they listened on a crystal set. There were only fifty or a hundred of these "amateurs" in the entire city.

My ambition was to go back to Savary, put a bunch of equipment together, and talk to someone not on the island. Isolation was something we all felt very strongly in the remoter places on the coast. The prospect of being able to break through the long winter silence with wireless was very exciting to me.

One day I happened to sell a twelve-foot work boat I had found on the beach and fitted with a small engine. I spent the entire 50 dollars sending away for radio parts. I got a pair of brown bakelite Montgomery Ward headphones and a galena crystal with a cat's whisker, and for the rest all I used was bellwire wound on a circular oatmeal carton to tune it. Equipped with this apparatus, I could hear ships and shore stations sending their Morse Code messages. I had weak reception but my friend Jimmy Anderson climbed a tall tree and got a huge antenna up. I'd stay up half the night after everyone else had gone to bed, learning to read the Morse Code and trying to tune in new stations.

One night in 1922, I was twiddling the controls when suddenly, I couldn't believe my ears. Music! We'd read about "radio broadcasting" starting up, but it was all very strange and far away. I listened and listened until finally I heard the announcer's voice: "This is K-P-O San Francisco. You are listening to Rudy Seager's orchestra in the Fairmont Hotel." I darn near died.

I got Dad out of bed. He listened to it, and the next night pretty near everyone on the island was crowded around our radio listening. This was the human voice coming out of space. It seemed unthinkable. And music. Played in San Francisco and heard in the same instant on Savary Island.

Once everyone got over the shock, they all wanted me to build *them* a crystal set. Harry Keefer, the postmaster and storekeeper, gave me $25. He said, "Build me the best one you can get!" I started building sets and selling them, just like that. By 1924 I had saved enough money to come back from the logging camps for good and go into business. Radio boomed, and it carried me with it. I often say I never worked a day since!

People began to come into Savary from all over. They got to hear about me and they'd come down in boats from Homfray Channel, from Teakerne Arm, from Refuge Cove—"Where's the radio man?" I had a real production line going, taking "store-boughten" sets that didn't work and rebuilding them. I was thrilled. To be able to stay home and make money just fooling around at radio seemed like getting it for free.

After a while I got to thinking that my market could be greatly extended if I could somehow get out on the water and take my services to the people of the coast. Up to this time I had just been sitting back waiting for people to hear about me by word of mouth and then find the time to make their way over to Savary and track me down. But there were lots of customers up every inlet and channel who wanted radio if only I could get to them, if only I could get a gas boat large enough to take me around.

For many years I couldn't afford a boat. Then in 1935, Frank Osborne, my machinist friend at Lund, told me about Eric Nelson, a retired Swedish fisherman who might let me use his old codfishing boat, the *Mary*. It was thirty-two feet long, wooden, with a 9 horsepower Buffalo engine. Eric agreed to let me use the boat, and in return I would pay him a dollar a day and keep it in good repair.

Now I was well and truly launched. The *Mary* opened up a whole new world of business. I began cruising up and down the coast, calling in at the logging camps and homesteads among the northern islands as far up as Loughborough Inlet. It was so much fun in those days, going around. Every little

The sand road on Savary shortly after we built it.

Previous page: **Looking from Indian Point across at the mountains up Homfray Channel.**

place had eight or ten families living in it. Before long I knew just about every logger, fisherman, and stump-rancher in the whole area.

Things were going so well that I decided to spend some money refurbishing the *Mary*. It cost me $700. But the job was hardly finished when Eric Nelson took the boat back and sold it for a profit. This left me with a bit of a problem. I had customers waiting for me, and there were rumours of another sea-going radio man setting up in competition, which he did in intervals between drunks. I had to find another boat in a hurry.

At this time I was a member of a group of ham radio operators living along the coast. We called ourselves the Island Net. One of the regulars was Bob Weld, a boatbuilding enthusiast in Parksville. He and his son had spent two or three years building quite a large power boat in his back yard. Compared to anything I had had, it was a veritable palace. Well, I was telling Bob about my troubles and he said why didn't I buy his boat. His son had joined the BC Police and moved to Victoria, and it was too big for the old man to handle alone. He was asking $2,500 but we worked out a deal where I would pay for it at one dollar a day. In October, 1936, I purchased the boat and registered it in Powell River as the *Five BR*, part of my first ham radio call.

It was a wonderful boat. In 1937 I was married and lived aboard with my wife; my eldest son Ronnie, born in 1940, spent his first two years on board. The *Five BR* increased my range so that I could travel farther up the coast, eventually as far as Seymour Inlet and the north end of Vancouver Island. For seven years it served as my office, workshop and floating home. It became well known in all the little camps, canneries, steamer stops, and stump-ranches, although few people referred to it by name. I installed a police siren which I would blow coming into harbour and everyone ashore simply said, "There's the radio boat."

We were by no means the only ones doing business from a boat in those days. There were quite a few "store boats" and agents of one kind or another selling hardware, clothing, dry goods, whatever any-one needed. Sea-going dentists, insurance salesmen and hairdressers, including ladies who did hair-dos for the women and, in some cases, more personal services for the men. We got to know them all.

When the war began, I tried to enlist in the Air Force but at that stage they were taking only university graduates so I concentrated on my radio work. I used Savary Island as my home address. Customers wrote me there or sent in one of the reply cards I had printed up. Mother would look at my calendar, see where I'd be next, then forward the mail there by steamer. It was a clumsy method. Sometimes it took several weeks to respond to a message. There were pieces of paper chasing me all over the coast, and it was working less and less well as business grew and steamer service declined.

There was a demand about this time for some sort of two-way communication along the coast. The first radiophones, supplied by the Canadian Marconi Company, came in around 1921 or 1922. They were as big as refrigerators. Only a government forestry launch had room to put the darned thing. The Marconi company had a monopoly—if anybody else built one, Marconi would sue. Finally a guy named Ed Chisholm began building and selling transmitters right under Marconi's nose and they couldn't stop him; when I saw him getting away with it, I started. The first one I made went into Theodosia Arm for the big Merrill, Ring and Moore camp.

Between running the *Five BR*, repairing household sets, and doing everything else, I was having a hard time keeping up. Once again the Island Net came to my rescue. Jim Hepburn, one of our members, was working as office boy and radio man for Island Tug and Barge in Victoria. I arranged with him to take over the building of my radio-telephone sets. Things went so well that I soon suggested he join the business. I had found I was missing out on a lot of sales because I was up the coast somewhere chasing my tail when the inquiries came in. I figured the best solution was to establish a base in Vancouver where Hep could direct traffic and build radiotelephones full time. We built a tiny box of a building at the foot of Cardero

The Roaring Hole at Mackenzie Sound, one of many tidal basins on the coast.

Street and early in 1941, Spilsbury and Hepburn Ltd. was born.

From the first, Hep was snowed under at the shop. We both worked incredibly hard for incredibly tiny sums of money. There were times when neither of us took our salary because the bank account wouldn't stand it. But the wartime economy of the coast was heating up and the business grew in spite of itself. Even with Hep building every spare minute, we couldn't make enough radiophones to keep up with demand, and in July we hired our first employee.

Business was booming, but what with various wartime restrictions it became harder and harder to travel up the coast in the *Five BR*. Towards the end of 1942, I left Vancouver and went on a seven-week trip in the boat. When I got back, the oil controller lowered the boom on us and we weren't able to get enough gas to make a meaningful trip. We were grounded.

Oddly enough, Canadian Marconi chose this exact time to enter the field with a boat of its own. We could have fought the ruling, I suppose. Or paid 5 dollars for a commercial fishing licence and disguised the *Five BR* as a fishboat.

Instead, I bought an airplane.

We started building the road up the hill from the wharf with just two wheelbarrows and a boom winch, no other machinery.

Terry Anderson standing beside the Model T Ford truck that we bought for road building.

IN THE TAXI BUSINESS

My dad and I built the first and only road on Savary, from the government wharf up to Indian Point. It was exactly 4.78 miles long, and we received the grand sum of $4,780 from the hotel people for building it. Now, for $1,000 a mile, you can't build much of a road at the best of times. There were lots of trees and stumps in the way, and we arranged to go around most of them. There was no money for surfacing, so the road was mostly pure sand. Cars with the old, hard, narrow tires tended to dig themselves in and get stuck. We found it helped to let about half the air out of the tires.

In 1927, after we finished the road, we helped to build the Royal Savary Hotel at Indian Point. For the road construction we had bought a 1926 Model T Ford one-ton truck, equipped with the largest Firestone tires we could buy. Then we bought a used 1923 Model T Ford touring car which we painted bright yellow. This was our taxi. We incorporated under the name Spilsbury and Son and waited for the business to roll in.

Quite understandably, the hotel felt that it should operate its own chauffeur-driven vehicle, a 1920 Franklin sedan. It was remarkable in many respects. The body was aluminum and the frame was aircraft spruce. It had a 6-cylinder air-cooled engine, equipped with a large fan, similar to an airplane propeller, that sucked in air under the hood and blew it back on the road under the rear of the car. This might be fine on a hard surface, but on a sandy road, and a dry day, the dust storm was something you'd expect to see in the Sahara. The chauffeur was a small, hard-working Cockney with a good sense of humour, and he needed it.

At first, all vehicles stood by on boat nights at the government wharf and when the number of arriving passengers was known they would be distributed accordingly. If there were five or less, they would ride in the relative comfort of the hotel limousine and their baggage, along with the groceries, would follow in our truck. Charge—$2. If there were more passengers, our yellow taxi took the overflow. Charge—$1.50. This worked out fine for us and it looked like the future of Spilsbury and Son was assured. However, the hotel management was not known for throwing their money around and steps were taken to cut back on some of the extra charges.

The Franklin sedan had running boards on both sides, ready-made shelves for stacking luggage. Someone contrived to attach expandable folding metal fences to the running boards, so that about four suitcases could be stacked on each side. The only drawback was that the passengers had to get in first, then the fences and baggage were deployed, and finally the chauffeur had to climb in through the window.

The next innovation was to construct a two-wheeled trailer, fitted with an enormous box, to tow behind the Franklin. This would take care of any additional baggage plus, in many cases, the groceries, milk cans, and blocks of ice that otherwise would have gone in our truck. No one could understand how the poor Franklin stood up to such overloading.

On one particular night, everything was going according to plan. The Franklin was full, the baggage racks loaded, the trailer heaped with cargo. Spilsbury and Son got only some extra passengers for the taxi, so I followed behind at a respectable distance to allow the dust to settle.

About three miles up the road, there's a short, steep hill with a sharp turn at the bottom, so that when you were going towards the hotel it was difficult to get much of a run at it. When I arrived with the taxi, there was the hotel limousine halfway up, and stuck but good. The back wheels were mired in the sand almost to the hubs. The little chauffeur had climbed out over the baggage rack and unloaded all the valises. He had disconnected the trailer and was in the process of unloading it. There was no way we could get past, so my passengers got out and we all set to work assisting the cheerful chauffeur.

The first thing was for everyone to push the Franklin up the hill, empty. The chauffeur had already asked his passengers to please get out and walk, but one of them, Mrs. R., a very prominent Vancouver society lady who under other circumstances would have arrived in the family's well-known steam yacht, obstinately refused. No way would she get out and get her fancy shoes full of sand. No one could persuade her otherwise, so we had to push the Franklin up to the top with Mrs. R. sitting in isolated splendour in the back seat. I recall she was wearing a fancy mauve dress with lots of sequins that glittered brightly, before they were covered with sand.

The chauffeur was a very ingenious man who didn't discourage easily, but that trailer must have tried his patience. Its sides were quite high, but the road was rough and any baggage casually tossed in would invariably get tossed right out again during the drive. So he had to tie everything down with rope. But this didn't always work. The rope would stretch and some of the bags would wiggle their way free, then bounce out onto the road where the next car would pick them up, if it could stop before running over them.

Well, the chauffeur came up with a solution. Not only did he rope them all down, he carefully threaded the rope through the handles of all the bags. For some reason he then secured the end of the rope to the clevis on the tongue of the trailer. One day we were

following close behind the Franklin, just far enough back so that the worst of the dust had settled, when we rounded a corner and had to pull up short. There in the middle of the road was the trailer, standing on its head, so to speak. The pin had come out of the clevis and the tongue of the trailer had dropped to the ground, stabbing itself into the road. So here was the trailer, both wheels about two feet off the ground and still spinning.

The trailer was completely empty. No baggage. The rope through the handles had looked after that. We didn't go very much farther before we found the first suitcase, minus handle. We picked up more and more bags, and by the time we reached the hotel, we had them all. And there was the chauffeur coiling up about forty feet of rope, with a bunch of valise handles on the end of it!

Grading the road with our Caterpillar tractor.

Unloading lumber at Indian Point for the construction of the Royal Savary Hotel, 1927.

The Royal Savary Hotel under construction. It stood until the mid-1980s.

The first wooden tennis court on Savary, which I helped to build. Judging by the number of spectators, a tournament must be underway.

Spilsbury and Son taxi service delivers a group of passengers from the wharf to the hotel.

The entire fleet of vehicles on Savary Island in 1931.

After we had the truck for a while, we realized we had to have something a bit better for passengers so I went to Vancouver to buy a good Model T touring car. At the same time, Allan Mace asked me to try and pick one up for him too, but $25 was as high as he could go. Well, this is Allan's $25 car.

Golfing at Indian Point on the "course" organized by the Royal Savary Hotel. You could only play at low tide. That's Mother on the left.

My mother perfecting her swing on the sand beach on the south shore of the island.

GOLF: AS I ENJOY IT

olf was a restricted form of entertainment on Savary Island, because the only place to play it was on the beach, at low tide. As a consequence, the other kids and I were able to find lost golf balls. You see, a golf ball will not quite float but will sort of slop around below the surface. With tide and wind, the ball will usually come to rest at the half-tide mark, a long stretch of beach where bits of sodden wood and seaweed collect. We collected quite a few balls with the help of my old English sheepdog, Pongo, who could find them like crazy. But we didn't really know what to do with them at first. Then one day, I found a golf club half buried in the dry sand where some people had been lying in the sun and snoozing between games. It had been there a long time and was getting rusty, but its performance was not seriously affected.

There was one thing wrong. It was a left-handed club, a putter. But it was iron, and I found that it made a pretty good all-purpose right-handed club. If I applied enough energy, it even worked reasonably well as a driver. So

we were in business. We swapped the club back and forth between us, and managed to find more balls than we lost.

The first time I played on a real golf course was an accident, like so many other things that have happened to me over the years. It was 1954, and I was attending a meeting at the Harrison Hot Springs Hotel. I was about to go into the hot pool to forget my business worries when my friend Bob Gayer grabbed me and suggested we go and play a few holes of golf. ''Bob,'' I said, ''you know I don't play golf.'' But he insisted.

When we met downstairs, I hardly recognized him. He had changed into his golfing outfit. He had the whole works—special golf shoes with spikes, golfing pants, a jacket that reached to his knees and opened up to display a collection of hardware which looked like a storefront on Main Street, dozens of pockets containing spare golf balls, dozens of tees of various lengths and colours, special golfing gloves, and a cap. Bob had only recently taken up the game and he believed in being prepared.

We went to the club rentals and after about fifteen minutes Bob had picked out so many clubs that he had to rent a cart to carry them. ''Now you go ahead and make a selection,'' he said. I picked out a short-handled iron putter and said, ''That'll do me just fine.''

I won the spin and prepared to tee off, but Bob stopped me right away. ''Not like that,'' he said. ''Here, let me show you.'' And he began to give me instructions. I stopped him. ''Bob, I hold a golf club the same way I hold a falling axe and it seems to work OK for me. If I held an axe the way you just showed me, I'd chop my legs off!''

By this time a small crowd was gathering and I was getting embarrassed. To the best of my ability, I socked the thing. I was amazed to watch it arch skyward and land just short of the edge of the green, then roll about twenty feet towards the hole. One more light tap and I dumped it in. Bob was thoroughly awed. ''You got a birdie,'' he croaked (whatever that is). His game went all to pieces after that.

My old sheepdog, Pongo, who I swear could understand the English language, and our cat, Ginger.

MAKING MUSIC

I adored "Uncle" Mick Hackney. He was artistic and played the violin and piano beautifully. He taught me to sketch when I was just five. As a professional soldier, a sniper, he served in both the Zulu and Boer wars before coming to Canada as a student farmer. In 1914 he joined the Anzacs and lost an eye at Gallipoli. Invalided back to Vancouver, he joined the 72nd Highlanders, went to France, and died at Passchendaele, August 1918.

Don't get me wrong. I am not musical in any sense of the word. I cannot read music or play music. I cannot hum, sing, or whistle a tune. But over the years, I have been exposed to it and enjoyed it in one form or another.

When I was very young on the farm at Whonnock, "canned music" had not yet made its appearance. Some people had player pianos, and most everyone played an instrument of their own. My mother played the violin and the double-bass; Dad played the cello; my Aunt Bess played the piano. Our next-door neighbours all played something—the cornet, the trombone, the flute, the clarinet, the banjo, whatever. One evening a week was devoted to music.

When we moved to Savary, we took all the instruments with us and in no time at all a different group formed. Again, one night a week was music night, usually in the dining room of the old Savary Inn in the off-season.

One year, about 1928 or so, my friends and I assembled a band. I use the term with some misgivings. The point, I guess, was to produce hand-made music for dances. Alice Mace played the piano. Her brother, Alan, played the clarinet. Hob Marlatt could turn his hand to almost anything, and I was elected to play the drums—a snare drum, a bass drum, and a pair of cymbals for emphasis. Believe it or not, the people over at Lund heard about us. They badly needed a live orchestra for their dances. They offered us $5 each to go over and play, and we jumped at it.

I remember one time in particular. It was winter. We went over in my small open boat, getting thoroughly chilled in the process. The dance was held in the dining room of the old Lund Hotel. All the chairs and tables had been moved to one end. It was well attended, Finns and Swedes ga-

lore. One of the favourite tunes was the "Dark Town Strutters' Ball," one of those pieces that builds up to a final crescendo, which ends with two deafening bursts from the drums and a clash of cymbals. I was running this part of the machinery and never quite knew when I was supposed to execute the crash. Hob would reach under the music stand and kick me on the leg and I would hit the cymbals. It seemed to work pretty well and the local people loved it.

I've mentioned that the weather was very cold. So cold, in fact, that one of the toilets in the men's washroom froze up. The staff pinned an Out of Order sign on the "men's," which was located immediately over the dining room. Later in the evening, when the party really got going, someone in a rush ignored the sign and flushed the toilet. Water poured through the ceiling, forming a small lake in the middle of the dance floor.

But the party went on; the Finns and Swedes simply danced around it.

In 1922, three of us boys spent five months logging shingle bolts up Homfray Channel. The closest neighbour was five miles away. We seldom saw a stranger in those days. One beautifully calm Sunday, when we were taking things easy, we heard something. It was Frank Osborne, the machinist from Lund, coming slowly up the channel in his boat, the *Mariposa*. Above the purr of the engine, we could hear a cornet. I never knew that Frank could play the cornet or had a musical bone in his body, but there it was, echoing off all the mountains, Frank playing "When Irish Eyes are Smiling." On and on and on. It went all the way up Homfray Channel and around into Toba Inlet when we could no longer hear it. It left a lasting impression on me. Even now, when I go up Homfray Channel, I can still hear the echo of Frank's cornet, playing "When Irish Eyes are Smiling."

The hotel in Lund where our gang was asked to make music. The dining room was on the other side.

My 1931 Plymouth, which I bought from Emil Gordon in Powell River for an old player piano, a set of encyclopedias in a wood case, and $100 cash.

Beachcombing during the
Depression, with Slim DuBerry
on the right.

Myself, Hob, and Allan setting
out on one of our
mountain-climbing expeditions,
in "Our Boat."

Allan Mace and myself on our way up Mount Estero in 1933.

My first flight was in this airplane, a Fairchild Razorback. One day in 1932, it appeared on the beach at Savary, flown by Grubby Grubstrom, quite a well-known pilot at the time. He agreed to take my two friends, Hob and Allan, and me on a ride around Mt. Denman. We had already tried to climb it, without success. Hob and Allan kicked in some money and I came up with the rest. It was probably around $25. So we took off. But with the three of us and the pilot, he couldn't get enough altitude to go around Denman. So we never did get up there. Grubstrom did take me up again to get a photo of Savary from the air. I had this old box camera and I'm hanging out the window trying to get a picture, but the wind is slamming the bellows shut all the time. Finally, I just held the camera out, snapped the picture and hoped for the best. When I was through, he said "Hang on," and he dived very steeply, then pulled up and did what they called an Immelman turn. You go up to the stalling position and fall off on one wing. Then he dove back down and went screaming down the beach about fifty feet above everyone's head. Just to show off. So that was my first ride in an airplane.

Grubby Grubstrom on the right; Ted Cressy on the left; Margaret Hutton posing in the middle.

Mount Denman from the air, 20 years later.

My ham shack in the corner of my bedroom in 1931. The tall piece of equipment is my ham transmitter.

Another view of my bedroom-cum-radio shack. The headquarters of my radio business.

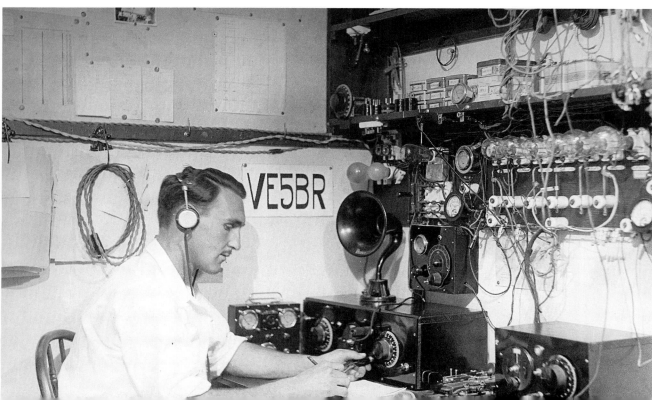

In front of our house, I erected this mast that carried my ham radio antenna.

About 1932, the latest thing in
ham radio was what we called
five metres. Here my dad and
myself are out on the end of the
wharf at Savary testing this
equipment.

Part of the same five metres
experimenting.

GOOD YOKES

In 1934, when I had just started going up and down the coast repairing radios, the Surge Narrows storekeeper asked me if I could do anything for an old timer who lived all by himself on a very small pension. An old radio was his only form of enjoyment since his eyesight had failed and he could no longer read. I had many such customers, and I tried to look after them without it costing much.

I went up to this fellow's cabin. His name was Isaacs. At a guess I'd say he was about 85 years old. Used to be a hand logger. After getting his radio perking again, I sat and listened to him talk about old times.

"Savary Island, I know Savary Island," he said. "How's old Jack Green? Good guy, Jack, always help a feller out, yep. And he made the best damned yoke in this part of the country, bar none. Sold them all over the coast, he did."

I asked him what he meant, vaguely associating the word "yoke" with an eggnog. He showed signs of losing patience with my ignorance, but then I guess he remembered I had just fixed his radio and not charged him for it. There must be some good in me. So he did everything but draw me a picture.

"Guess yer too young to know, but a yoke goes around an ox's neck and hooks up with a coupla chains for pulling logs in the woods. They gotta fit just right or the animal can't pull proper, and they gotta be goddamn strong too for this kinda work. That's where he had it all over the others. He made his yokes out of yew wood.

Them yew trees grow all along the south shore of that island right at the top of that sand cliff. I used to give him a hand sometimes and go over and cut some of them yew trees and pack them down for him. Christ them things are heavy, and have you ever tried to saw one? They'll take the teeth right offen a saw like it was cast iron."

So now I knew the story behind the many large stumps of yew trees I had seen just behind the cliff edge on the south shore. And I wouldn't mind betting that most of those stumps are still there after all this time. That yew wood hardly ever rots.

I asked Isaacs if he knew that Jack Green had been murdered. He said he guessed he heard something about it. "Too damn bad. Jack was a good guy just the same."

The *Mary*, my first radio boat, after my renovations.

A "Macfarlane boom" at Myrtle Point, south of Powell River. Brooks, Scanlon and O'Brian logged there before Powell River even came into existence. This photo was taken in the 1930s. It's all residential now.

A typical A-frame logging outfit somewhere on the coast, serviced by the *Five BR*.

The Palmer Logging Company operation in 1932, eight years after I worked for them. The donkey was the same one I used to run. The men are setting chokers at the foot of a spar tree and tight-lining logs down to the water. This spot in Johnstone Strait is now called Palmer Bay.

The Union Steamship boat *Chelohsin* at Stuart Island Landing in the 1930s.

The store and post office at Blind Channel in Mayne Passage, where Sidney Boardman ran the show. I used to go up regularly and fix his radio. Mrs. Robarge lived in a floathouse just to the right of this picture. She kept chickens, which used to come ashore on a boomstick to feed on the beach. She was very bow-legged. Anyway, one day she came ashore and while she was away a cougar went out the boomstick to get at the chickens. Then Mrs. Robarge returned. According to Sid Boardman, the cougar and Mrs. Robarge passed on the boomstick, and there was only one way it could be done—the cougar went between her legs!

Indians gambling during a potlatch at Quathiaski Cove, 1932.

Stuart Island Landing, on one of my radio visits. The building on the left is the store, run by the Wilcox brothers.

The *Five BR*, our home away from home for several years.

The radio boat in Bute Inlet. We sent out this photograph as publicity to all our customers.

My mother and I in 1936.

My mother was always getting animals, then leaving my dad and me to take care of them. This was one of her "pets," a black horse she got from Mr. Daniels, the postmaster at Cortes Island.

Aunt Bella in 1936, during her visit from England, with my mother and dad.

Refuge Cove, 1937.

Olas Lea at his place in Agamemnon Bay in 1937. He was the fellow who was building the boat that my parents were planning to use to cruise the coast before my dad went broke at Whonnock. Later he moved up here near Earl's Cove where he continued to build very good boats.

My dad admires the view at Port Neville during one of my radio visits.

Twin Isles, a private yacht owned by R.M. Andrews.
He was a mining engineer who made a lot of
money in Japan. But he could see the war coming
and he wanted a place to live until it was over. He
bought Twin Islands, just off the south end of
Cortes Island, and lived there for the duration of
the war. His log cabin there had ten bedrooms, and
I got the job of putting a radio in every one!

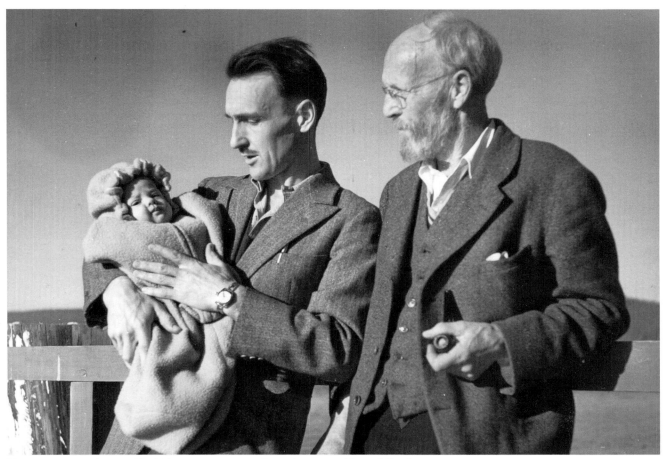

Three generations of Spilsburys—my son Ronnie, myself, and Dad.

On Christmas Eve in 1940, the Union Steamship
Lady Cecilia went aground in Pender Harbour. I
happened to be there and jumped in my boat and
went across to see what I could do. But it was no
use. It took a tug from Victoria at high tide to get
them off. I sold this picture to the Vancouver Sun
for five dollars.

The Gilford Island Indian village, Gwayasdums, during a visit in 1941. The old fellow is drying fish and cedar bark. Today it is really the only occupied Indian village in that part of the coast. All the others are abandoned.

My first wife, Glenys, and Ronnie on the *Five BR* at Gilford Island, 1942. There were eight or ten longhouses still standing when I used to go there during the war.

House posts at Gilford Island, 1941.

Right: These grave posts were in a place we called Burial Cove, just around the corner from Gilford Island village.

Tree burials at Gilford Island.

Below: Inside a decaying longhouse at Gilford Island.

The original Vancouver headquarters of Spilsbury and Hepburn at the foot of Cardero Street in 1941. Contract price complete—$1500 borrowed.

My first partner, Jim Hepburn, and his dog Sparky. Everyone knew Jim simply as "Hep."

In 1945, Jack Tindall bought into the company and it became Spilsbury and Tindall. Here he is with his daughter, Margaret.

During the war, I sold the old *Five BR* to a guy who ran a machine shop down at the foot of Cardero Street in Vancouver. He fixed it up and at the end of the war he sold his shop so he and his wife could go up and down the coast in the boat selling something or other. He put in a full-length bathtub for his wife where I used to have a radio room. He later sold it, and after that I lost track of it. Then, in 1956, I came across it lying beside the wharf in Earl's Cove where I got this final picture of it.

CHAPTER THREE
Running an Airline

I called my second book of memoirs *The Accidental Airline*, and that about sums it up. I never expected to get into the flying business. I just thought that having an airplane would eliminate all that chugging around the coast by boat at seven miles an hour. It would open up the radio business and keep us one step ahead of the competition. Well, we got the plane all right. And the next thing I knew we were running the third largest airline in Canada.

The airplane was my cousin Rupert's idea. He was my Uncle Ben's son, a few years younger than I. He was a test pilot for Canadian Pacific Overhaul and there wasn't much he didn't know about flying. Listening to us complain about not being able to get up the coast on business, Rupert suggested we buy an airplane. According to him they'd all been grounded by the war and we could pick up one cheap. He made it sound as though we couldn't afford not to.

The idea was not entirely new to me. I had an interest in planes and a couple of flights along the coast had got me thinking how much easier our work would be if we had one. It was hard to justify leaving the office for months to float around doing installation and nickel-and-dime repairs up the coast, when the deals were being made in the city. What I needed was a way of getting out and back on installations more quickly. When the oil controller shut down the *Five BR*, the time seemed right.

Rupert found a plane for sale in Montreal, a Waco Standard four-place biplane. The owner, Albert Racicot, was a bush flyer closed down by the war. We got him to bring his price down, and he even agreed to deliver the machine to Vancouver. I raised the down payment on a life insurance policy and somehow wangled the necessary permits to allow us to fly the wartime skies when nobody else could.

Meanwhile, where was the plane? First the floats arrived by rail, then the skis. Eventually we received a telegram from Princeton. Racicot had got that far but the sight of the Coast Range had competely unnerved him. He'd never seen clouds so full of rocks before. He had fourteen children and a wife in Montreal and he was going home. So he left the key with the station master and boarded a train. Rupert found the plane under a tree.

Our first flight was on January 4, 1944, taking a complete radio-telephone station to a camp up Salmon Arm. We were twenty-five minutes in the air each way, a trip that would have taken two full days each way by boat. It was like travelling in time. I recognized that flight could be a huge boon to the people of the coast, and once again, as in radio, I had the feeling I was uniquely positioned to give it to them.

The plane really helped our radio work and we kept growing in that department. But we also very quickly got into the charter business. We just hadn't imagined how much demand there was. There was no commercial flying on the coast at that time, so with all our contacts in the logging and fishing industries, we were overwhelmed right from the start. They wanted our radios, but when they saw the plane we brought the radios in, they wanted the plane even more. Overnight the airplane was pulling in more revenue than the radio business.

Another thing the plane did was extend our range. Using the boat just hadn't been practical for going any farther afield than the north end of Vancouver Island. But with the plane, the whole coast as far north as Prince Rupert was our beat.

The plane itself was just about the best sales gimmick I'd ever had, especially up there. People were just amazed to have anyone come all the way up from Vancouver to see them. Once they saw the plane, Marconi didn't stand a chance of getting their business.

At the end of the war, we got a charter licence and even made a stab at flying a scheduled passenger service between Vancouver and the Queen Charlotte Islands. That time the inspectors shut us down. But early in 1946 a group of big logging companies with sites on the Queen Charlottes gave us a contract to provide steady air service to their camps. With their backing we were able to buy a couple of twin-engine Stranraer flying boats and convert them for passengers. In June we incorporated a new company for the

The Salmon Glacier up behind Stewart, BC.

flying side of things. We settled on the name of Queen Charlotte Airlines Ltd. (QCA).

By this time we'd been running a de facto passenger service into Prince Rupert for a few months. We weren't licenced for this and every flight had to be disguised as a charter of some kind. Finally we screwed up our courage and applied for a licence to fly a scheduled service, Vancouver-Prince Rupert. The application was heard by the Air Transport Board in February, 1947. It was opposed by Canadian Pacific Air Lines, which wanted the service itself. Grant McConachie had big plans to make CPAL a trans-Pacific carrier and the Prince Rupert run was part of the deal.

After the first day of the hearing into our application, things looked to be going our way. Then McConachie came waltzing over and made me an offer I couldn't refuse. If I withdrew the Vancouver-Prince Rupert application, he would give us all their licences on the south coast. These were rated as Class 1 scheduled licences. It seemed like a wonderful deal. The south coast was where all the people were. It was a compact flying area we could handle nicely with the kind of equipment we had. After lying awake all night thinking about it, I decided to accept.

Queen Charlotte Airlines was now a major scheduled airline. When the figures came out for June 1949, only Trans-Canada Airlines and Canadian Pacific had flown more revenue miles. All of a sudden we were the third largest operation in Canada, and we maintained that position by a wide margin from then on.

And we were still in the radio business, though I left this mostly to Jim Hepburn and Jack Tindall, another ham operator friend who had bought into the company in 1945. The aviation business now required my full attention. In the post-war period the coast north of Vancouver boomed to a degree that is hard to realize now. Almost every little inlet and cove had a camp in it. Places like Minstrel Island, Alert Bay, Tahsis, Zeballos, those were our mainstays. Gold River was opening up and the East Asiatic Company was going in and getting big. When you go up the coast now, all you can see are scars on the hillside

where the camps used to be, and there's nobody around. We were there when they were all booming and we couldn't help but boom along with them.

Finding new aircraft to put into service was always a challenge. We never had much in the way of capital, so when it came to new equipment we could only look for bargains. We became so expert in the purchase of used planes that we set up a separate company, Western Aircraft Sales and Service Ltd., to buy and sell equipment. The profits from this helped finance the airline.

Of all the Queer Collection of Aircraft we came to own in the course of our bargain-hunting, the one thing we're most remembered for is the gangling Stranraer. As time went on we became pretty embarrassed about the Strannies. We were never so proud as the day we graduated to DC-3s and left the old flying boats behind us. But the DC-3s just made us like every other airline. The Strannies had made us unique. Of all the planes we flew, they had the most personality by far.

The fun part of the thing was between 1946 and 1950, when we were collecting a good team of people and the company was doing nothing but go ahead. The real hard work came in trying to mould this ragtag bunch of obsolete aircraft and unruly, ex-air force pilots into a state-of-the-art airline. The new aviation industry, as it was then emerging, was no place for individualists. Pioneering a route or flying a daring rescue mission to some isolated outpost, you had to be a free spirit, but that's not what we were doing any more. We were grinding back and forth over scheduled routes. Everything was the same every day. It takes a different personality to deal with this kind of flying. It takes a person who can follow procedures, double-check every detail, stay within a wide margin of safety at all times and maintain unvarying habit over long periods of repetitive work. It isn't easy, and it's anything but exciting. It's why the old rugged individualist of the bush-flying era had such a hard time adjusting to the modern era of airline-type flying.

Acquiring the CPAL Class 1 scheduled licences in

Moss-covered trees along the plank road between Masset and Towe Hill on the Queen Charlotte Islands.

This is the road itself, c. 1947. We were up there making a good will tour of the area with Dr. Bill Kergin, our company doctor at Prince Rupert and a well-known medical man on the north coast.

1947 was a turning point. Meeting the Department of Transport (DOT) requirements for this class of service required a drastic change in our thinking, and a costly change in our day-to-day operations. The Air Transport Board (ATB) was formed by the federal government after the war to regulate and assist the orderly development of commercial air transportation in Canada. The DOT retained control of technical requirements. I had to begin spending a great deal of my time in Ottawa co-ordinating all this at head-office level. My diary lists over forty cross-Canada flights during the next eight years.

While the DOT set very high safety standards to apply to all Class 1 carriers, the additional operating costs were supposed to be offset by the ATB granting these carriers a monopoly over their licensed routes. So we had every assurance that our costs of upgrading would eventually pay off handsomely. And we were assured that the federal government wanted to encourage the economic success of all six Class 1 carriers in Canada.

For the first year or so it was nip and tuck—we just managed to break even—but there was one very important plus factor missing. In spite of our best efforts over the years we never managed to get a proper air mail contract with the Canadian Post Office. I spent eight years calling on the Post Office in Ottawa to apply for an air mail contract, but George Herring, the Postmaster General, simply said he had changed his policy. He would no longer subsidize air transportation, it would have to stand on its own feet in the future.

All other Class 1 airlines in Canada got a very substantial proportion of their total revenue from the Post Office. If we had received a similar deal, there would have been no need for the federal government to subsidize us, as it did in 1954. In fact, if we had received average mail pay from our inception in 1947 we would have been several hundred thousand in the black by then.

In the last couple of years of QCA's operation, an entirely new problem arose. The Aluminium Company of Canada started to build its large complex at Kitimat, and it looked like a godsend to us. Hundreds of people and thousands of tons of air freight had to be flown from Vancouver to Kitimat and Kemano, all over our existing Class 2 route up the coast. In order to cope we bought two PBY Canso Aircraft for our fleet. It looked like Kitimat was going to put us in the black. But we hadn't counted on Russ Baker.

Baker, of Central BC Airlines, had a small Class 4 charter operation based in Prince George. Without any licence to operate on the coast, he started to fly small aircraft from Vancouver to the Alcan site. The ATB warned him to stop, but he managed to get a contract with Alcan to fly freight and passengers. The ATB did not approve the contract, but Alcan overruled them on the strength of a special agreement it had with C.D. Howe and the federal government. Alcan insisted that the work should be open to all carriers, then gave Baker what amounted to exclusive rights to the flying. Meanwhile, we had to keep flying our daily schedule to Kitimat, despite the fact that we were often flying empty aircraft. Economics finally forced us to suspend service.

To add to all this, Baker started to raid our Class 1 scheduled points, such as Minstrel Island, Alert Bay, Zeballos, and others. On the way back from Kitimat he would have his empty planes stop in at our bases and pick up passengers waiting there for our flights, offering them lower fares to fly with him. We reported all this to the ATB and it sent Baker letter after letter warning him, but he paid no attention. Alcan was on his side, and Alcan was too big for the ATB.

With Baker's competition and no proper mail contract, things looked bad for QCA. Then Baker came to the end of his Alcan contract and, in order to survive, he tried to take us over. Right about then the Canadian DEW Line project was announced. We got on the bandwagon and landed a contract, and within six months we were making more money than we'd ever seen before. I figured that by the end of 1955, we would have paid off our debts and been right out in the clear.

However, that's when Baker, now Pacific Western Airlines, raised his offer. If it was up to me, we never

The Waco at Nootka cannery on one of our first charters.

would have sold. The trouble was, it was no longer up to me. I'd been selling handfuls of stock every time I got up against the wall and I was now a minority stockholder. There was nothing I could do about it. I kept myself busy running the airline and left the negotiations to others. In July, 1955, QCA was sold to Pacific Western for $1.4 million.

Looking back, I can't complain too much about the sale. My partners forced it on me, but PWA had offered a price they couldn't refuse and I couldn't have asked them to turn it down. I went back to the radio business full time and was just as glad to have some time to sit back and get my breath.

As for the little airline I started by accident back in 1943, it did pretty well for itself too. Under PWA colours, it went on to conquer the West. It did even more than that: thirty years later it opened its mouth, swallowed CP Air and became the second largest airline in the country.

On the **Salmon Glacier**, the cabin that never stayed in the same place for long.

The tractor rolling across a deep crevasse in the glacier. These were bigger potholes than I had ever seen, even on the Savary road.

GLACIERS

Getting our first little airplane gave us an entirely new perspective on the coast. It really shrank distances. And in one very specific sense, the Waco arrived on the scene just in time to "save our bacon."

We had received an order from the Dominion Government Telegraph and Telephone Department to construct and install a chain of radiotelephone base stations on the coast at such places as Bamfield, Winter Harbour, Coal Harbour, Masset, Port Simpson, and Stewart. As well, we were going to have to install countless small, low-power feeder stations at smaller communities and camps. This was a forerunner to the much larger network of stations that the BC Telephone Company eventually developed. Most of these places were served only by weekly steamer. For a single job, we might be faced with three days up, one week on the job, and three days back. The airplane made the whole job much simpler.

I will never forget my first visit to Stewart. It was a different world, a magnificent world of mountains and glaciers. I had never seen a glacier before, and certainly never expected to spend several days living on one.

We had shipped all the equipment up to Stewart by steamer ahead of time. Then my cousin Rupert flew me up in an easy day's flying from Vancouver, with a stop at Prince Rupert. I checked into the Stewart Hotel while Rupert went on to Ketchikan to await a phone call to return and pick me up. Simple, providing everything worked.

After taking about three days to install the main station in the Post Office, I was ready to install one of the feeder stations in a cabin up the Salmon Glacier. The cabin belonged to the Morris Summit Gold Mines. The only way to get to it was on a tractor train that roared, squeaked, and slipped its way about twenty miles up the centre of the glacier.

In Vancouver I had met the owner

Main Street, Stewart, 1944.

of the mine, Colonel Thompson, who had made it all sound quite easy. At Stewart I met "Ruddy" Rutherford, the mining engineer in charge. He was something else again, one of those characters whom nothing stops. If it's possible we can do it; if it's impossible, it just takes a bit longer.

The last time anybody had looked, the mine building was about halfway up the glacier. But by their very nature, glaciers are always on the move, and as they move they tend to open up large cracks and fissures which are sometimes concealed beneath the snow. These openings can be wide enough to gobble up an RD-8 tractor, as we were about to find out.

We found the cabin intent on heading downhill. We pulled it back and levelled it, and I installed the radiotelephone, battery, and small generating plant. But how to erect an antenna? Using some lumber that was scattered about, I managed to put up a couple of 2x4 masts, guying them back to posts driven into the snow. With the antenna stretched between the masts,

I was able to contact the base station in Stewart, and to talk to other stations as far south as Comox and Alert Bay. "Ruddy" was impressed.

When the sun came up in the morning, however, it thawed the snow around the masts and they both fell over. Re-erecting the masts became a daily routine, a task made more difficult by the fact that the cabin itself moved off in different directions each day.

Then there were the ice worms. I had heard old timers talk about them and I thought they were just kidding. But there they were, in the hundreds and thousands, just under the surface, wiggling and happy. They are about one to one and a half inches long, just like a very small angleworm, but black.

The cabin was small, only about 15 by 20, but it had the basic necessities, including an oil stove, and we passed a cozy night. In the morning, our tractor broke through a snow crust and sank into a large crevasse from which it could not be extricated. It was going

to be necessary to get a second machine, equipped with a winch, to recover the first one. This was arranged by radio. But what about me? My job was done. ''Ruddy'' said that I could walk back in half a day without any trouble by following another glacier and trail that would take me out to Hyder, Alaska. With a plane waiting for me, I took off down the trail with nothing but my tool kit.

Fortunately, the weather was good. The path followed the Salmon River and was all downhill so I actually enjoyed the experience. I passed the Premier Gold Mine, and for several miles I tramped along beneath a cable supported on towers, which was carrying huge ore buckets down to sea level at Hyder.

Hyder is connected by road to Stewart. There was no customs office, but there was a hotel of sorts, actually a whorehouse run by a well-known madam, and a well-patronized bar. The barkeep was a teetotaller, but managed to get drunk every night just the same, just serving his customers and getting into the spirit of things. On occasion he had to be carried to his bed.

I hitched a ride back to Stewart and phoned Rupert in Ketchikan to come and pick me up. While waiting, I stayed in the town's only hotel. But I had my choice of restaurants, both run by Greek gentlemen. There was ''Greasy Mike's,'' known for fried food, and ''Concrete Mike's,'' noted for pastries. I was surprised to see railway tracks leading out of town. Later I learned that years ago, the then-premier of British Columbia, Duff Pattullo, had plans to make Stewart the terminus of a transcontinental railway.

Flying over the Salmon Glacier to Morris Summit Gold Mines.

Bridging a crevasse with a board.

This ornate stove in the lobby provided central heating at the hotel in Atlin. A pipe ran to each room.

Making a flying visit to Rivers Inlet Cannery in the Waco.

QCA's first hangar at Vancouver Airport.

In 1948, the Fraser River flooded and we were kept busy flying in stuff to the farms and isolated villages. Here we are manhandling a load of hay onto an aircraft.

Flying in blood plasma to communities cut off by the flooding.

Paul Lake, north of Kamloops. This was during the
Fraser River floods, flying supplies into Kamloops
because the rail service was out. That's our
Norseman on the left. On the right is a Junker.

The *Chelohsin* at Sullivan Bay.

Sullivan Bay from the air.

When we were originally planning our flights from Vancouver to the Queen Charlotte Islands and Prince Rupert, we needed a refuelling point halfway up. For various reasons, Sullivan Bay was perfectly suited. We proposed this to Standard Oil, which then agreed to put in fuel tanks and floats and got Myrtle and Bruce Collinson to run it. The O'Brien Bay post office moved over, and that was the beginning of Sullivan Bay.

Right: The waterfront at Sullivan Bay.

One of our Dragon Rapides refuelling at the Bay.

TO THE QUEEN CHARLOTTES BY AIR

In September, 1949, I flew up the coast to Butedale to meet Louis Potvin, our service manager at Spilsbury and Hepburn. He was repairing a radiotelephone there and needed transport to Prince Rupert and the Queen Charlottes for other radio jobs. By that time I had learned to fly, sort of. On the way up I had a little mishap at Oscar Johnson's logging camp in Seymour Inlet. The end result was that when I took off from there I was flying a different plane, a rented Cessna 120.

The Cessna was a very small, under-powered machine, only capable of carrying a pilot and one passenger in the best conditions. After a takeoff run that used up half the length of Seymour Inlet, I finally got airborne. At Butedale, I picked up Louis Potvin and managed to get back into the air, with the help of a brisk head wind and because by that time I had burned off a lot of fuel. We reached Prince Rupert at nightfall.

Next morning, with the aircraft checked over and refuelled at our base in Seal Cove, Potvin and I climbed aboard and attempted to take off. Nothing doing. There was no wind to help, and nothing I could do got it unstuck. I kept trying in every direction and finally ended up down near Port Edwards, off the mouth of the Skeena River, where we found a little breeze. Still no go.

The plane felt funny. It seemed to list to starboard. I asked Potvin to look out his side, and he said that the nose of the float was right under water. I got out, removed an inspection cover, and found the front compartment of the float full of water. No wonder we had trouble taking off. This plane had no radio, so I couldn't talk to base. I pumped out the water and tried again but still couldn't get airborne. We taxied all the way back to Seal Cove and had our engineer look at it.

The front compartment had filled right up again. There was no sign of float damage, or any sign of where the water was coming in. Then the engineer removed the entire rubber buffer from the nose of the float and found a crack that opened with water pressure whenever the aircraft taxied. After this was repaired, we tried again. Still no success. Finally, by draining most of the fuel from the tanks, removing all our personal baggage, including Potvin's tool box, and practically stripping down to our underwear, we coaxed the plane into the air.

With greatly reduced fuel range, I was in no position to second-guess our crossing to the Queen Charlottes, especially since we had no radio and no means to call for help if we were forced down. So I climbed and climbed until the plane wouldn't go any higher—up to 8000 feet, I think—then headed across the strait, hoping I had enough altitude to glide to a coast line, or at worst to dump it next to a fish boat if I had to. Potvin was very nervous in airplanes, especially small ones. He needed constant assurances that this whole performance was safe. I said, "Heck, look at all those hundreds of little airplanes flying around Vancouver, flown by all kinds of clowns, and you hardly ever hear of one getting into serious trouble." (Charlie Banting, our superintendent of maintenance, used to say, "Them small airplanes will just barely kill you!") I told Louis to look out his side window for boats in Hecate Strait. He wanted to know why, and I said they might be good customers for a radiotelephone.

We made the crossing without incident and landed at Masset, where we tied up for the night at the QCA dock. One of our regular scheduled flights had brought over our baggage and tools from Prince Rupert that morning. By carefully trimming our fuel load, we managed to make the short hops to Port Clements, Skidegate, and Cumshewa and concluded the radio work. Then it was time for the return trip to Prince Rupert.

Sending our baggage on ahead, we waited a couple of days for just the right weather. Finally, when everything looked promising, we took off, assisted by a fresh westerly blowing up Masset Inlet. Because of the heavy chop running in the entrance to the harbour, I took off in the lee of the point, and in the teeth of a 30-knot gale, climbing slowly without making too much headway. At the mouth of the inlet, at 2500 feet, the engine coughed a couple of times, and stopped dead.

There were heavy waves in front of us, so I did the unforgivable. I turned 180 degrees downwind to reach more protected water, using up every last bit of glide I could afford before turning into the wind and setting down in the less-rough area near the beach. But even here the swells were unpleasantly large for a small plane. We hit the first one with a loud BANG, and both doors flew open. The rest of the airplane seemed intact. I tried the engine again, and to my surprise it started without hesitation. The wind was so strong that I couldn't turn the plane down wind, so I eased it out to the middle of the channel, shut off the engine, and "sailed" it backwards to the boat harbour and the dock. All this time Potvin was remarkably silent, not a normal condition for him.

The engineer removed the cowlings and did a thorough check of the little engine. He found nothing wrong. Nevertheless, he agreed to come with me on a test flight. Everything went well until we reached the magic 2500 feet, when the engine promptly quit again. We tried to restart it on the way down; nothing doing. But after landing on the water it started. The engineer worked on it all night and the next day we test flew it again, with exactly the same result. Quit cold at 2500 feet.

By this time there was nothing that would have induced Potvin to go up again. Quite truthfully, I wasn't happy at the thought of attempting Hecate Strait again myself, not in this aircraft. We caught the next scheduled flight out to Prince Rupert, and then back to Vancouver. It had taken eleven days to complete what was normally a three-day trip.

We told the rental company where it could find the airplane. They said not to worry, and sent up someone to fix whatever little thing had gone wrong, sorry for the inconvenience. It turned out the plane was up there for a long time. They had no better luck with it than we did. Eventually the engine was shipped back to Vancouver by steamship and another shipped up.

To the best of my knowledge, Louis Potvin never flew in a small aircraft again, at least not with me.

The QCA mechanic at Masset, just before giving up on the temperamental flying machine.

Two QCA planes, a Canso and a Norseman, arrive in Ocean Falls in the snow, a nice change from the usual rain.

Oscar Johnson, on the left, and his wife Maude, at their logging camp in Belize Inlet.

My spectacular arrival at the Johnsons' float, six inches short of the gasoline tanks. That's Scotty Graham, one of our mechanics, who was in the passenger seat at the time. This was the inauspicious beginning of the flight that eventually ended with us marooned at Masset. All decked out in my new Rayban airforce-style dark glasses, I could hardly see the water surface and ended up landing on the float on the second bounce. I never wore sunglasses again!

One of our Stranraers waiting offshore at Minstrel Island for passengers to be ferried out by boat.

Downtown Anyox.

QCA aircraft picking up passengers in Anyox harbour.

Left: Minstrel Island, as it looked in 1949.

PLANS FOR A PARK

Several times in the early years of QCA, we got charters to fly people in to Garibaldi Lake with seaplanes. Our pilots came back with glowing reports of the magnificent scenery so close to Vancouver. They insisted that I take an opportunity to go in and see for myself. In 1947, when we were asked to fly in a member of the mountaineering club, I went along for the ride.

I was quite unprepared for what I saw—heavenly blue and turquoise lakes, towering granite and volcanic peaks, lava beds that still looked hot, two huge glaciers. I never got over this first impression.

After a second trip in, during which we camped and hiked all around the area, I got all fired up and decided we just had to do something about it. I wanted to bring Garibaldi to world attention by flying people in to a spot which up until then could only be reached by the hardy few who made the full day's climb up from the railway station. Garibaldi was a provincial park reserve, so I went to meet the parks board.

The chairman, Dr. F.C. Bell from Shaugnessy Hospital, and Harry Graves, the secretary, were active members of the mountaineering club. They were very much in favour of providing controlled access to the Garibaldi Lake area. It was something they had wanted to do on their own but never had the funds to accomplish. Air transportation seemed to be a practical approach, provided the airline financed it. We were prepared to go along with them if we could get certain tenure and protection. We laid on a full day's trip for the board and assorted dignitaries in one of our Stranraer flying boats, and a contract was drawn up.

The agreement was that QCA would build a cabin on the lakeshore large enough to handle ten visitors. We would outfit the cabin, operate it

This was my first flight into Garibaldi Lake. For some reason, Bill Peters, right, is dressed like he is going to a wedding. You can tell he's the pilot; he's the one wearing dark glasses.

Dr. Bell, chairman of the parks board, helping to start a fire before leading us on our first climb up the Black Tusk.

during the open flying season, and provide regular air transport on a "per seat" tariff, which we had already arranged with the Air Transport Board. Within three years we were supposed to provide additional accommodation for ten more visitors. In return, we got a lease on a small piece of property on the lakeshore, adjacent to the Battleship Islands, on which to erect and operate the "Airline" lodge. We also got exclusive privileges to provide air transport to the lake. The contract and lease were for twenty years, renewable for another twenty.

Once the agreement was signed, we lost no time in going ahead with our plans. The property was surveyed, the site was cleared, a small dock was installed, and we began flying in loads of lumber with our big flying boats. The cabin was built during the late summer of 1949. It was very sturdily constructed, two storeys

A Stranraer arriving at Garibaldi Lake with a load of lumber to build our cabin.

with a steep, corrugated aluminum roof. There was an oil stove and rudimentary plumbing with a septic tank.

In the first two or three years we flew many planeloads of passengers in and out, and engaged the services of a fabulous coastal character, Red Mahone. Red was an Irishman, a one-time logging camp and towboat cook. He stayed in for the flying season, operated the radiotelephone for daily weather reports, cooked wonderful meals, and had a story for every occasion. I can still picture Red in his cook's apron, bare hairy chest and arms and shiny bald head, standing over twenty people at the rough cedar table loaded with his cooking, and shouting, "Come on, you bastards, eat what's on your plate or you'll get

My son David on Table Meadows, Garibaldi, carrying a man-sized pack.

it in your hotcakes in the morning.'' Visitors loved it.

Local weather conditions made it difficult to maintain reliable air service in and out of the lake. When Vancouver was enjoying clear weather, Garibaldi might be plugged with solid cloud. Many flights had to turn back, and in one instance we lost a Norseman seaplane on its final approach to the "Barrier" under a low cloud ceiling, when a violent downdraft put it into the trees in Rubble Creek. Miraculously, no injuries, but the pieces of the aircraft are still there. It was a great help having someone like Red in residence at the lake with a radiotelephone, because he could give pilots up-to-the-minute weather conditions. I recall one very professional-sounding exchange. Vancouver dispatch called Garibaldi for an update on the weather. Red came back, "She's fine, come on in." Being cautious, the dispatcher said, "OK Red, but what is your visibility?" Red's reply: "Visibility? Hell, I can see further than I can look!''

Ice was another problem. Some years ice remained on the lake until early July and left us with a very short flying season. Because of the attractive skiing conditions in the winter and late spring, we had a real need to provide winter transport and we tried to come up with a technique for landing float-equipped aircraft on snow. After many adventures, we were forced to the conclusion that helicopters were the only aircraft that could do the job, and in those days they didn't build them big enough.

It got to the point when, under our agreement with the Garibaldi Parks Board, we were supposed to build a second cabin at the lake. At the time, prefabricated Panabode dwellings

The view from our cabin, looking past the Battleship Islands at the Sphinx Glacier.

were becoming popular, so we asked their engineering department if they could come up with a design that could cope with the snow-load conditions at Garibaldi. They assured us they could. We were surprised to see that they proposed a roof structure providing very little pitch, when our other cabin had a pitch like a church steeple. Don't worry, they said, they would guarantee that their structure would handle the load. That convinced us. We bought the whole kit and we had the cabin up before the first snow came.

We proudly advised the parks board, and the members said that as soon as the lake opened the following summer they would like to go in and inspect the cabin. About mid-July, 1952, we made the inspection trip. The lake was free of ice, but there was still a few feet of snow on the ground. And we found absolutely no sign of our new cabin, just a shallow hump in the snow where the previous fall it had stood two storeys high.

You wouldn't believe the mess we found when the snow melted. There was not a single piece of timber—rafters, joists, or siding—that had not been broken into pieces about four feet long. It looked like a giant bulldozer had crawled over it. We didn't see enough salvageable wood left to build a decent-sized dog house. I took some photographs and went back to see the Panabode people. They agreed to replace all the material at their cost, about $3500 as I recall, and this time they would put our kind of roof on. I pointed out that the cost of flying it in to the site would equal or exceed the cost of the material. That was our tough luck, they said. They wouldn't accept transportation charges. We never did resolve the matter, because a new set of circumstances intervened and Panabode got off Scot-free.

In 1953, after the Social Credit party won the provincial election, I

had a visit from someone who said that he represented the Provincial Lands and Forests Department and that under the new government, Garibaldi Park had been taken over "by the Queen" and the old Garibaldi Parks Board was no more. They would appreciate our not carrying out any more work on the project until the situation was clarified. When I pointed out that we held a perfectly legal contract which would have to be assumed by the Crown, he agreed and said that if we rendered a statement of expenses we would be compensated fully.

I should have got it in writing! When I submitted our complete costs, about $13,000, I asked that we have an early decision as to the government's intentions. We were in the process of replacing the second cabin at the lake, a project that would involve quite a bit of further expense. The representative said he would get us an answer as soon as possible, meanwhile he advised us not to do anything more at the site.

We waited and waited, but heard nothing. I began to wonder if the government realized what it had in Garibaldi Park, so I prepared a detailed brochure with photographs describing the story of the lake and our part in developing it. Then I made an appointment to meet Premier W.A.C. Bennett at his office in Victoria. Bud Lando, our legal counsel at QCA, came along with me. But the premier didn't show up for the meeting, and the official who did show up knew nothing about the matter.

Finally, after more waiting, word came from the government—a brief letter from Ray Williston, Minister of Lands and Forests. He stated that it had come to his attention that QCA had a contract with the Garibaldi Parks Board and that as of such and such a date, which was two days before the letter was written, QCA had failed to comply with the terms of the agreement. He explained that we had been required to build a second cabin, that we had not done so, and that we had thirty days to remove all our materials and so on from the lake. The contract with the parks board was considered null and void.

I was so mad I wanted to sue the government, spill the story to all the newspapers, do something, anything, to publicize what was happening. But Bud Lando pointed out that "you can't sue the government." Anyway, he argued, we will probably be asking them for some business in the future and this would ruin our chances. Cooler heads than mine prevailed, and we never collected anything from the government for all our efforts there.

That was in 1954. In 1955, we sold the airline, and I haven't been back to Garibaldi since. I guess I should go, since I left my outboard motor, sleeping bag, and parka hanging in the cabin.

On a flight into Garibaldi Lake in 1951, Johnny Hatch crashed into the trees below the Barrier. He was carrying these three young women, who planned to do some climbing in the mountains. As you can see, they emerged from the wreckage unhurt. In fact, they seemed rather pleased with the adventure. Maybe they thought we did this for all our passengers.

Opposite, top: Our first cabin sees its first snowfall.

Opposite, bottom: Disaster strikes! Our professionally designed second cabin in all its glory. It collapsed into a pile of broken lumber under the weight of the snow. So much for engineers!

FALLING OFF TABLE MOUNTAIN

About the time we were first getting excited about flying in to Garibaldi, Carl Agar was starting to make a name for himself as the "father" of commercial helicopter flying, particularly in bush transport and mountain work. We were good friends and he rented part of a QCA building as the maintenance depot for his Okanagan Helicopter Co.

Carl developed a method of operating helicopters in mountainous terrain at altitudes well above the posted operational ceiling for machines of that day. For instance, a chopper could fly to 5000 feet, and even manage to hover at 5000 feet, but if it landed, it couldn't take off from that height. It needed some flying speed. The way Carl overcame this was to sit the chopper down on a ledge with a sheer drop-off in front. He would get his rotor spinning in flat pitch at maximum revolutions, then slam it into climbing pitch and "jump" the machine off the ground. But he jumped sideways, so the copter fell off the edge of the cliff. Down it dropped until it gained flying speed so that it could resume normal flight.

He was looking for a place not too far from Vancouver where he could train his pilots in this technique. He told me he was going up to Garibaldi to try Table Mountain, which looked ideal. It was 6600 feet high, with a nice flat top and a clear drop-off of a thousand feet.

Carl picked a clear day, no wind. He and his mechanic flew in to Garibaldi, carefully sized up the ground, then landed gently on top and shut off the motor. Getting out to stretch their legs, they had a smoke while they planned their course of action. The area was perfect in every way—quite level, smooth, and grass-covered, like a football field. Then he walked to the edge and looked over. He was never so scared in his life. It was the height that got to him—it took him half an hour to steady his nerves. But the jump went as planned, and I believe they used the spot many times afterwards.

DOWN THE DAISY LAKE TRAIL

I flew in to Garibaldi one weekend to do a little work on the cabin. Johnny Hatch (our pilot), Dick de Blicquy, and our secretary at QCA, Audrey Garard, joined me. We were going to spend some time Sunday walking up to the meadows and the Black Tusk.

We got an early start up the hill, packing just a light lunch and my camera. The meadows were covered with a profusion of wildflowers, the air sweet with their scent. The panoramic view of the mountains and snowfields was overpowering. Then Johnny voiced an overpowering preference for staying where he was. He did not like mountain climbing, and he wanted to go to sleep right there among the flowers. He suggested that Dick and I go ahead and climb the peak; he and Audrey would wait for us.

This sounded OK at first, but there was a hitch. Johnny calmly announced that the little Stinson aircraft they'd come up in could not take off at this altitude with three passengers. Someone would have to stay behind and wait until the next aircraft came in, or walk out to Garibaldi station and take the train, which operated only three days a week. Since one person could not stay alone, and there was no other choice open to us, Dick and I "volunteered" to remain behind.

Eating our sandwiches in silence, we contemplated our choices. At that time there was no stock of food in the cabin, and no radiotelephone. Accordingly, we decided that after climbing the peak, Dick and I would walk out to civilization. Why not? People had been doing it for years, hadn't they? I was a bit annoyed that Johnny didn't seem impressed by our gallantry. I have a sneaking suspicion he had planned it this way all along and had simply saved the bad news for the end. We took our leave, wishing the others a pleasant sleep, and headed up the mountain. One thing in our favour—we were travelling light.

After climbing around the peak, we circled down to Taylor Cabin and the start of the trail to Garibaldi Station. For the first mile or so the trail was well blazed and easy to follow. Then it opened into a small alpine meadow no one had used this year. The meadow was overgrown with flowers that obliterated the track. Dick explored to the right, I explored to the left. Finding some tree blazes and the trail, I turned to shout to Dick, who was by now about a quarter of a mile away. Apparently he didn't hear me. He waved down the hill, yelled, ''I found it!'' and disappeared into the trees at a gallop.

I waited for him to reappear, but he was on his way, stopping for nothing. I guess he didn't want to miss his train. Then I made my mistake. I followed him.

The trail Dick had found was obviously a very old one. There were some blazes on the trees but they were almost covered over with new bark. There were numerous windfalls across the path, some of which had lain there for years. I tried calling but couldn't make him hear me. Half an hour later, about two miles down the mountainside, I caught up to him. He had lost the trail and was trying to clamber down a steep rock face.

While I caught my breath, I told Dick in no uncertain terms what I thought of his poor display of woodsmanship, running on ahead like that. But what to do now? It was a long, slow climb back up to the meadows, it was getting late, and we were tired. We made the wrong decision—to find the old trail and continue on.

The trail was becoming harder to follow. Blazes were few and far between. Fallen trees obliterated the path for long stretches. In one place we found several old, rusty mink traps hanging on trees. The trees were so dense that we could not see out. We were very hot, and extremely thirsty. There were no creeks or springs and the woods were very dry. Finally we lost all contact with the old trail. The mountainside became less steep. Now we just struggled straight through the heavy undergrowth, with lots of devil's club and vine maple clinging to us.

We were growing quite discour-

My secretary, Audrey, Johnny Hatch, and Dick de Blicquy in the meadows shortly before we went our separate ways.

aged when we came out into a clearing in which there was a small log cabin and some farm sheds. We climbed through the wire fence and made our way to the door. An elderly man, who I took to be Scandinavian, was bottling beer at an outside table. He didn't seem a bit pleased to see us and wanted to know what we wanted. To say the least, he looked incredulous at our story. We must have been following the Daisy Lake Trail, he told us. It hadn't been used for years. In fact, he had lived there for over twenty years and we were the first to come down it in his time. He was deeply impressed by our mistake. Later we found out that the Daisy Lake Trail is about three times as long as the Rubble Creek Trail, having been surveyed originally on a 10 percent grade as a wagon road.

The man's wife brought us water,

then he showed us to the trail, which we followed for a mile or two down to the railway track very close to the Daisy Lake station. When we asked someone when the next southbound train would be coming, he said, ''in about twenty minutes.'' With only three trains a week, how's that for timing?

While waiting for the train, Dick and I each consumed a quart tin of orange juice without stopping to gulp. Then we rode out through the spectacular canyon in an open passenger car. There was a warning sign saying that the company was not responsible for injuries to passengers from falling rock.

At Squamish, we walked down to the dock and boarded the Union Steamship *Lady Alexander*. We must have been a pitiful sight. Our clothing was torn. I had lost almost an entire

The Black Tusk, which we climbed before our descent down the Daisy Lake Trail.

leg of my pants, and half the sole of one of my shoes was flapping. We were smeared with charcoal from coming through some burned-off areas, and covered with dried blood from numerous scratches. But we were the happiest two passengers that ship had ever carried. The *Lady Alexander* got us into Vancouver in time for supper. I phoned Johnny, but he wasn't home yet. Guess he took my secretary to dinner.

Our first overnight camp at Garibaldi Lake. Mike de Blicquy with his dog, and Corporal Roy Allen of the provincial game department.

Previous page: **Two of the Strannies refuelling at Sullivan Bay.**

Right background, one of the main life-boat stations on the west coast of Vancouver Island, at Tofino. Two of our Norsemen are at the dock, along with my little Stinson.

A Canso PBY at the airplane float, Alert Bay. We bought our first Canso in 1951.

Mrs. Kenmuir, QCA ticket agent at Alert Bay, in about 1950.

Our mailbox outside Mrs. K's door.

In 1952, we took a flying trip all around northern BC with the MP for Skeena, Ted Applewaite. We were hoping to win his support for QCA in our battles with Ottawa. This is a view of Ketchikan.

Ted Applewaite, in Ketchikan, during our tour.

On the same trip, we stopped overnight at Telegraph Creek and slept in the jail.

Creek Street, Ketchikan's red light district.

Our plane moored in the Stikine
River in front of Telegraph
Creek.

One of our pilots, Sheldon Luck
(right), taking some Alcan brass
into Kemano. The man in the
centre is George Williamson,
public relations manager for
Alcan.

Our beaching ramp and seaplane dock in the middle arm of the Fraser River, about 1952.

Left: One of the Strannies shortly after it hit a deadhead landing at CeePeeCee on the West Coast. No one was hurt, but the plane needed a new bottom, its fourth.

One of our Dragon Rapides after an unorthodox landing on Digby Island in 1949. Pilot Roy Berryman is reluctant to take leave of his command. Someone had siphoned off all Roy's fuel, and when both his engines conked out shortly after leaving Prince Rupert, he had to come down in the trees.

Left: The Strannie pulled up on the beach at high tide for repairs at the CeePeeCee cannery.

CF-CRS, our first and favourite Norseman, meets an ignominious end. BC's infamous coastal weather claims another victim. How can you land on water you can't see? This "renowned" pilot flew the Burma Hump for two years. He lasted two weeks with QCA.

Even on the ground our planes could get into trouble. This one capsized in the Fraser River when the snow became too heavy on its wings.

High and dry at Tofino, waiting for the tide to come in so we could take off. We played noughts and crosses in the sand for four hours while we waited. That's the Stinson, which I used more or less as my personal plane.

This one wasn't my fault! Someone lost control of our jeep and put it down in a ditch.

The Cessna Crane, with which we tried to launch a scheduled passenger service to the Queen Charlottes. The DOT did not smile on this attempt.

Now we were an airline! Two of our DC-3s at Vancouver airport.

Our attempts to fly into Garibaldi in the winter were generally successful. It was flying out again that gave us the trouble.

One of the Mark V Ansons that we sold to the government airline in Ecuador. They bought about six of them, and before six months were up they had wrecked every one of them. The airports down there were so high that even empty the planes would have a job taking off. The way they overloaded them, they'd simply take off and crash.

At sea level, we found we could land on and take off from a snow surface quite easily on floats. This is my little Stinson at Cassidy Airport in Nanaimo.

In my office at the airport, about 1954.

Bud Lando, our lawyer and the airline's vice-president, at the Seaplane Terminal, Vancouver airport.

When I was learning how to fly, Rollie Barrett was one of my instructors. She was one of only four female pilots in those days. She worked for us at QCA for a while.

A Staggerwing Beech at Savary Island in 1950. This was going to be my private airplane, but it turned out to be a tricky thing to fly on floats and I didn't keep it.

CHAPTER FOUR
Back to the Coast

After the sale of the airline, all my interest in aviation came to an abrupt stop. I deliberately tried to put the company out of my mind. I threw myself into the radio business, which was growing fast and badly needed a headquarters with more floor space. With part of the proceeds from the sale of QCA, I bought an old red brick warehouse on Cordova Street and converted it for our requirements.

The building was constructed in 1901 as a livery stable. It was owned by the largest cartage firm in the city—the Vancouver Transfer Company. The main floor was all wagons. The second floor was horses, with an inside ramp for them to walk up. The top floor was all hay loft and there was a six-foot gap in this floor so hay could be pitched down into the mangers. The second floor had two troughs running the length of the building so that all the manure would run out into the lane at the back.

When I bought the place, there were over one million baled gunny sacks stored in it. The most recent owner had bought empty grain sacks, vacuumed out the residue and sold it for pig feed, then repaired and resold the sacks. The top floor was wall-to-wall sewing machines with matronly operators working under dim, dusty, bare light bulbs. The inside finish was whitewash and horse manure. We couldn't clean it off, so we covered it with gyproc. It took six months to convert the building, but Spilsbury and Tindall operated in it for the next thirty years.

The company grew steadily, specializing in designing and building some very sophisticated single side band (SSB) radiotelephones and selling them all over the world—Europe, South Africa, South America, Cuba, the Orient. By the time I sold the company in 1981, it was one of the largest exporters of SSB equipment in Canada.

But my struggles with the federal government didn't cease, nor did my trips to Ottawa. I was still battling the Department of Transport—the radio communications division this time. Because of the prevailing lack of recognition of the West by eastern Canada, I spearheaded the formation of the Western Canada Telecommunications Council (WCTC) to make our voice heard and to defend the interests of the West. When I retired from the WCTC in 1982 I was honoured with the creation of the Jim Spilsbury Award, given annually to the person who contributes the most to marine safety through the use of radio.

During this time, I found myself hankering after another boat so I could get back to the coast that I had known for so many years. With some cash in my pocket from the sale of QCA, I could afford something larger and more comfortable than the *Five BR*. I searched the waterfront looking at everything available, but after three months I'd found nothing to my liking.

Then my old friend Captain Hudson, rumrunner-cum-boat salesman, told me he had found exactly what I wanted, a boat called *Blithe Spirit*. She was only seven years old. Her owner and builder, Tom Fenner, was setting off to travel Europe for a few years and was going to lay her up. He had received several offers, but he refused to sell to anyone he didn't consider worthy. The boat had just gone into storage at Burrard Yacht Club, but Captain Hudson persuaded Tom to let me see her. He took off some of the tarps and I crawled in to look her over. It only took me ten minutes to make up my mind—this was the boat for me. Tommy warmed up to my enthusiasm and agreed to sell. He even knocked the price down several thousand for cash. He left everything aboard—kitchen dishes, blankets, china, even the ship's binoculars—the whole works. I wrote a cheque and he gave me the keys. I met his wife Molly and she cried. They certainly loved that boat.

I've been touring the coast in *Blithe Spirit* ever since, for both business and pleasure. In October, 1956, after I'd owned the boat for a year, I decided it was time to demonstrate to everyone at Spilsbury and Tindall that *Blithe Spirit* was a great asset to the company's sales and marketing division. So a business trip was arranged, four of us on a twelve-day cruise from Heriot Bay to Simoon Sound. We covered 330 miles and made sixty-four business calls, stopping in at stores and logging camps, machine shops and

The interior of Spilsbury and Hepburn's first radio shop on Cardero Street in Vancouver.

From Cardero, we moved our headquarters to this establishment on Water Street.

canneries, post offices and sawmills. Surge Narrows, Stuart Island, Thurlow, Blind Channel, Grassy Bay, Beaver Creek, Port Neville, Call Creek, Turnbull Cove, and many more. Going back over that route today I would have difficulty finding more than ten points of call with more than a dozen people in them—a striking example of how the coast has changed in my lifetime.

When I was just starting out, I dreamed of providing improved communication (radio) and improved transportation (air transport) to the coast. I thought it would make life easier for the people who lived there. Well, things didn't work out as I expected. It turned out I was simply part of a process that saw the coast slowly depopulated as people moved away to make their living in the cities. Nowadays the world I knew has all but vanished. As I cruise the bays and inlets I have known so well, the coast for me becomes a haunted place, haunted by all the people and places that gave it life.

For all the changes, however, the most important things remain the same. We still have the ocean, the mountains, the rocks, and the forests. These things have not changed or gone away, and they remain a source of constant pleasure for me.

For all the ghosts that inhabit it, Spilsbury's Coast is still the best place in the world.

Inside the Water Street factory in 1952.

Our factory on Cordova Street, originally a livery stable.

Jane Day testing frequency control crystals in the shop.

Inspecting some of our famous SBX-11 portable radiotelephones. In production over twenty years, they went to the North Pole and to the top of Mount Everest, and they're still going strong.

An Australian sheep herder using a Spilsbury radiotelephone. Our equipment sold all over the world.

Shortly after we sold the airline, I purchased a bunch of these Isetta cars to sell in Canada. It was a German design, built in England. I met Count Halvel from Germany, who told us about this wonderful little car that was going to change the whole face of the automobile industry. He persuaded us to get in right at the beginning and take it for Western Canada. Pretty soon they were arriving by the freighter-load, and we couldn't stop them. We hired Staff Plant (on the left in this photo) as the manager. Johnny Hatch, our old pilot, took about forty of them to Hawaii where he hoped to rent them out to people who wanted to drive around the beach. Staff sold fifty to an oil man in Edmonton. Then we had to begin practically giving them away. When we got all through, I'd lost about $65,000. I remember somebody sending me to see this smart young guy who was just starting up in business. He was in charge of the used car department for one of the big motor dealers—Jimmy Pattison. I was hoping he'd take them all off my hands, but Jim looked them over and he wouldn't touch them with a fifty-foot pole. Even then he was smarter than I was! This photograph shows a few that we used as radio service vehicles. That's Louis Potvin, sales manager at Spilsbury and Tindall, on the right.

ASLEEP AT THE WHEEL

When Tommy Fenner sold me *Blithe Spirit*, he spent some time showing me the various pieces of equipment and safety devices. I was very impressed with one arrangement. He had installed a quick-change type of valve in the suction line of the engine's raw water pump. One way it brought water in to cool the engine, but in case of hull damage, or an excessive amount of water in the bilge, you just had to swing a lever over and it pumped about twenty gallons a minute out of the boat.

Tommy then told me in considerable detail about the time he sank *Blithe Spirit*.

He was coming back from a charter trip to Alaska with one person on board, his cook. Southbound in Seaforth Channel at about midnight, he had been at the wheel for twelve hours and was getting woozy. He only knew he'd fallen asleep when he woke up to discover that he'd hit a steep rocky bluff head-on, doing 10 knots!

When he picked himself up off the deck, he saw that the boat had bounced back and was about to take another run at it. Tommy threw it into full reverse and backed away. Part of the bow was gone, and the focs'le was filling with water forward of the engine room bulkhead. He looked at the clock and remembered that only minutes earlier he had turned on the searchlight and noticed a small bay and gravel beach to starboard. He turned around, located this beach, and ran the boat right up on it.

Then Tommy ran down into the engine room to switch the raw water pump over to the bilge. By the time he had done this, he was unable to open the engine room door against the rising water in the focs'le. He was trapped in the engine room. There is a large hatch in the floor of the wheelhouse that lifts up to give access to the engine. But when he tried, he couldn't lift it. The cook was sitting on it, and the cook was a fairly fat man. He had the radio in his lap and was calling Mayday, which was pointless since all the wires had been torn off and the radio had come off its shelf and catapulted to the front of the wheelhouse. Tommy lay on his back, got his feet against the hatch, and finally managed to dislodge the cook.

The tide was rising, so they both stayed up all night working the manual bilge pump. When daylight came, they saw a fishing boat passing by. To attract its attention, Tommy fired two shots across its bow with a rifle. He said the third one he was going to put right into the boat, but the fisherman finally noticed and came in to them. There was nothing he could do, but Tommy asked him to go to Butedale, about twenty miles down the coast, and get a couple of seine boats up to salvage *Blithe Spirit*. This they did. One boat on each side with ropes between them cradled her and took her down to Butedale for temporary repairs. Tommy said the shipyard there did such a good job that he was able to continue to Vancouver under his own power. At Vancouver Shipyards the forward part of the boat was completely rebuilt: new bowstem, new keel, new deck, and new planking for twenty feet back.

Moral: Don't go to sleep at the wheel. Any time I am running at night, I do not use the wheelhouse chair. I put it out of reach and pace back and forth to make sure I don't doze off.

Blithe Spirit in about 1958.

This is Doris Hope's house in Refuge Cove. She is my sister-in-law. In 1945, the Hopes bought out Jack Tindall, who operated the store up there. With the money he got from the sale, Jack joined Spilsbury and Hepburn, and after that it became Spilsbury and Tindall. This particular house used to be up Teakerne Arm, where the Murrays lived in it. They looked after the booming grounds for the Powell River Company there. Before that, it was one of the houses built for the construction crews that built Powell River in 1910. After the construction period was through, many of these houses were sold and people towed them up and down the coast. There are old Powell River houses all along the coast, and this is one of them.

Back to the radio business in 1956 after selling the airline.

100 PERCENT SAFE—ALMOST

During the first year that I owned *Blithe Spirit*, I installed some new electronic equipment, including a very good depth sounder that recorded on a paper roll. I planned a trip up to Refuge Cove, by myself and non-stop. After I left Vancouver, a thick fog settled in, reducing visibility to fifty yards. I had to navigate on compass headings and running time, blowing my air whistle every three minutes as required. It didn't particularly worry me; I had operated like this for years with the *Five BR*. I hit Merry Island and Welcome Pass right on, enjoyed a brief glimpse of the shoreline, then went back on compass. The depth sounder ran continuously, providing a contour chart of the bottom for the entire 100-mile trip. By checking this against the fathom contours on the marine chart as I went along, I could double check my "blind flying" position.

Somewhere off Pender Harbour, a tug with a tow of logs appeared in the fog. He called me on radio and asked for a position report; he hadn't seen land for many hours. I gave him my calculated position and he thanked me, saying his own radar had broken down. Clearly he did not realize that I didn't have radar at all!

Back in Vancouver, I showed our purchasing agent the rolls of recordings I had made on the trip. He was most impressed, especially since it was he who had found and purchased the sounder for me. He asked me to show the chart rolls to a group of his boating friends at their next meeting, where they were studying navigation. It turned out to be the Canadian Power Squadron. At that time the Vancouver squadron had eight members. After I parted with my $10 fee and passed my entrance exam in June, 1957, I became number nine. From then on I became deeply involved in CPS. Captain William Yorke (Bill) Higgs, with a lifetime operating tugs on the coast, taught us

safety. "If you hole your boat," he used to say, "don't abandon it. Stay with your vessel, plug the hole from the inside with anything available—cushions, blankets, tabletops. Keep 'er afloat 'til help arrives." His teachings reached thousands through CPS and saved many boats and lives.

Eventually I became an instructor, and in 1969 I wrote and published a new piloting manual which was used by many squadrons across Canada. Vancouver Power Squadron now has a membership of over 400.

Another group active in marine safety and rescue was the Towboat Owners Association, which formed after a nasty accident. One stormy night in December, 1953, the tug *C.P. York* hit a reef in Welcome Pass, rolled over, and sank. Five men lost their lives; two miraculously survived. The tragedy was that the captain of the tug had had several minutes before the vessel sank to radio a Mayday—and no one answered. Two other tugs were tied up in Secret Cove only two miles away, but the crew had switched to the broadcast band to listen to a hockey game.

That's when Captain Cy Andrews persuaded the Towboat Owners to take action. From that time on, all tugboats were required to listen 24 hours a day on the emergency channel (2182 KHZ in those days), and the Department of Transport ordered that the broadcast band be removed from all radiotelephones. The boats' crews responded with enthusiasm, with the result that we soon had a coastwide fleet of at least 700 tugs, manned by experienced seamen, standing by and ready to go to the assistance of any boat in distress. It was the best equipped and largest fleet of coastguard vessels the coast has ever seen.

All this was in full swing when I bought *Blithe Spirit*, and I lost no time getting involved. We installed one of our little AD-10 radios in the control

room of the Second Narrows railway bridge in Vancouver. The bridge attendant guarded the radio and was able to talk to boats all the way up the coast. At the same time, he was in 24-hour telephone contact with Captain Andrews and his search and rescue effort.

I felt that pleasure boats should contribute their services as well, so in 1958 I joined with Dr. Bob McKechnie of the Royal Vancouver Yacht Club to form the Gulf of Georgia Searchmasters Association. The Department of Transport in Ottawa presented each of us with a certificate and an official Auxiliary Coast Guard pennant. I still carry mine in *Blithe Spirit*'s flag locker. Our rules were simple: any time the owner was aboard, the vessel must have its radio tuned to the emergency channel and its pennant flying. This situation remained in effect for several years, until Ottawa got into the act by forming the Coast Guard Service.

By this time I was so deeply involved in all aspects of marine safety that *Blithe Spirit*, of all vessels, should never find itself in trouble. We had enough equipment and knowledge aboard to cope with every imaginable situation. So the incident I am about to relate must be the exception that proves the rule!

We were at our place in Ballet Bay on Nelson Island, enjoying a quiet weekend. We had set our string of prawn traps off the mouth of Blind Bay the night before. Now there was a heavy cloud buildup and although the weather was calm, I had a feeling we might be getting a blow soon. I thought we'd better pick up the traps before it came. I headed out with Staff Plant, my friend, and Dud Meakin, my partner.

We already had our trap line on the windlass and the first trap on its way up—when it struck. I have seen "line squalls" before, but never one like this. There was a line of white spray right across the horizon, with curtains of heavy rain, almost black, behind it. It was approaching us at about 40 mph and before we could dump the trap line, we were in it. In two minutes we could not even see the shore line half a mile away.

Staff wanted me to go in a little closer because he was trying to take a photograph of the spray and wind and waves as a subject for a painting. The sounder showed only one fathom under the keel. And then we felt four bumps—not hard, as though we were bumping on a sunken log. When I got out into deeper water, Dud said he thought he'd better stick his head into the engine room and check for water in the bilge. ''Sure, go ahead,'' I said, ''maybe we're sinking! Ha! Ha!'' He came back and said, ''I guess we are. The floorboards are all floating!''

Sure enough, we had about two feet of water forward of the bulkhead. I ripped up the carpet. Apparently there was a hole on the starboard side, behind the permanent plywood panelling. Using a chainsaw I had on board for just such emergencies, I cut away all the panelling on that side. The hole was punched through the bottom between two ribs. It was about six inches across and water was squirting in. I yelled for someone to pass me a blanket to plug the hole. Dud arrived with a pillow from one of the bunks, which he stuffed into the hole and stamped on. A bit too hard. The pillow casing burst and disgorged thousands of little foam rubber pellets. But it did seal off most of the water.

In the meantime, I got Staff on the wheel and told him to head full bore down the channel to our place, where there was a small bay with a clam beach. I just hoped we would make it before the water reached a level where it would stop the engine.

In the engine room, the water level

In **Blithe Spirit's** wheelhouse, showing some of the equipment that made her accident-proof, almost.

An aerial view of our place at
Nelson Island.

was about two feet above the floor-boards. There were three smaller holes in there, but under the engine where I couldn't plug them. So our water-tight bulkhead was serving no purpose. I got to the valve on the raw water pump and swung it over to work as a bilge pump. That sucked out twenty gallons a minute and gave us a little time. Besides that, we had two automatic electric bilge pumps and an emergency fire pump, all soon working to capacity. By now there was about a foot of water in the after cabin, and it was gaining on us rapidly. There was nothing more to do, except hope. It was touch and go.

Then the alarm bell started ringing. The engine was overheating. All those foam rubber pellets had spread through the bilge water and plugged the intake screens of every pump, including the big one on the main engine, so the engine was not getting any cooling water. The fresh water in the heat exchanger was boiling and squirting steam. The exhaust manifold glowed a dull red and the rubber muffler was melting. I had to get out of the engine room because of the steam and smoke. We made it through the gap in the boom and just as we slid up on the beach, the engine quit. We had three feet of water above the floorboards, bow to stern.

I got on the radio and called the *White Wing*, the camp boat at Milligan's Logging Camp in Vanguard Bay. I told him our problem and asked to borrow his scow pump. He was there with the pump in half an hour.

In the meantime I got a large tarpaulin. We carried it on board and rigged a ''tingle,'' or ''collision mattress,'' by putting ropes on the four corners and pulling it over the bow and under the keel until it covered the holes in the hull. The outside water pressure sealed it tightly against the hull and practically stopped the leaks. All we had to do now was pump a few

thousand gallons of water out of the hull! Even with the scow pump, it took several hours.

The next problem was to position the boat over a part of the beach that was relatively level and smooth so that when the tide went out that night the hull would come to rest where there were no large boulders. This entailed rigging the anchor cable and two long lines from the vessel to the shore, and holding her in position against a violent wind that reached 35 to 40 knots at times. Comox Coastguard Radio was busy handling five separate Mayday situations with vessels in trouble all over the coast.

As the tide fell we got her heeled over so that when she settled she would expose the damaged, starboard side. We went up to the work-

shop and got a piece of plywood. We sealed the outside of the hull with a Hudson's Bay blanket folded in three and soaked with a gallon of marine paint, then nailed on the plywood to cover the holes. When the tide came in, the boat floated and didn't leak a drop. By this time, the batteries were dead and the auxiliary plant and main engine were both damaged beyond repair. With the lifeboat and outboard motor, we towed *Blithe Spirit* off the beach into the next bay, where we waited for Captain Len Higgs and his tug, *Sechelt Chief*. He took us in tow to the shipyards in Vancouver.

Six weeks and $85,000 later, *Blithe Spirit* was as good as new. But our long list of mandatory safety precautions now includes suitable reference to foam rubber pellets!

Blithe Spirit, **beached on Nelson Island, with four great holes in her bottom.**

THE LARGEST SPRING

According to the ship's log book, it was May 1, 1959, when *Blithe Spirit* departed Vancouver with about half a dozen people on board, including two or three from the factory. We were just abeam of Point Grey when we picked up a Mayday. The Norwegian freighter *Fern Gulf* was on fire and in distress off Point Atkinson. Captain Andrews of the Towboat Owners got on the air and asked all vessels to go to its assistance. The fire was spreading and the ship was dead in the water. We could see the crew throwing burning objects overboard, including furniture and lumber. The Vancouver fireboat had been requested, but the authorities would not let the boat go outside the First Narrows.

We approached very slowly in case there was anyone overboard. Suddenly, our engine stalled and *we* were dead in the water. I could start the engine again, but when I put in the clutch, it stalled. There was something in the wheel. I launched the dinghy and got alongside. With a boat hook, I reached underneath to see if I could free whatever it was. I hooked into something, but every time I pulled on it I could get it to come only a couple of feet before it would pull me back again. Whatever it was was jammed solid and we were helpless.

At length, a tug took the freighter under tow and the other ships departed. I meekly called Captain Andrews, who was in charge of the rescue operation, and asked if I could get a tow into Vancouver. The tug *Arctic Straits* offered to help, and we were ignominiously towed back through First Narrows into the harbour. I had already radioed my mechanic, Les Ashton, and alerted him to the situation. By 11 p.m. we were hauled out on the ways at the Royal Vancouver Yacht Club where our problem immediately became apparent. We had run over a large coil spring mattress that was floating just below the surface. The whole thing had wrapped into a ball three feet in diameter around our propeller and rudder, jamming everything hopelessly.

Next morning, it took Les three hours with a cutting torch to cut it all away, spring by spring. Each one would snap free and knock his mask and goggles off. His language was unprintable. We reported to the insurance company, which sent an inspector down. Captain George King of the Western Marine Underwriters surveyed the situation. He advised that we could proceed on our trip, but at the earliest possible date we should be hauled out and get permanent repairs done. He concluded his report with the words that in his opinion, "this is the largest spring ever caught in the Gulf of Georgia."

The *Blithe Spirit* with an entire mattress spring wrapped tightly around its propeller.

SOLITARY LOGGING

When I bought *Blithe Spirit* from Tommy Fenner he made me promise one thing. He had some very good customers from the United States who chartered the boat every year for a trip from Vancouver to the head of Knight Inlet and back. He promised them that they could still use the boat under its new ownership. I readily agreed, although I was not really interested in the charter business. Tommy put me in touch with these people and a date was set.

Five of us left Vancouver: my friend, Staff Plant, on board as cook, the three Americans, and me. The next day we were in Knight Inlet. My passengers asked me to stop at a small logging camp at Axe Point, warning us ahead of time that they had known this man for a long time and that he was something special.

His name was Bill Baker, and he owned and operated the logging camp all by himself. That didn't mean that he was a hand logger, though there were lots of them around. This man used machinery; he used a logging donkey, he used spar trees and high lead and even a skyline. It was something to see and hard to believe.

He had a Fordson tractor logging donkey on top of a hill, about 800 feet above sea level on a steep bluff, and he had a well-rigged spar tree. He felled and bucked the trees himself, and with the high lead method he yarded them in and piled them at the foot of the spar tree. Then he took his mainline, brought it down to the beach, hooked on to a ringbolt in the rocks and used it as a tightline. He climbed up the steep hill—something that would take an ordinary person a good hour—and put a choker around the log. Then he started the engine and tightened up the line, and the log went screaming down into the water. He shut down the engine, climbed back down the hill, ran out the boomsticks to unhook the choker, climbed back

up the hill, restarted the engine, and hauled the rigging back up for the next load. He'd been doing this for months and had several sections of logs in the water all boomed up.

Even more extraordinary was the way he had moved his donkey engine from the top of another hill about a thousand feet away with a steep canyon in between. "I tightlined it across," he told us. Sure enough, what he did was to go over to the new hill where he rigged a spar tree, then pulled the line across, which meant going down into the canyon and back up the other side. He rigged his mainline from the top of one spar tree across the canyon to the top of the other spar tree; in other words, a skyline. Then, using its own power, he hoisted the donkey on its sled off the ground to a block on this skyline. He had already taken the haul-back line across to the new setting, so when he had the donkey hoisted off the ground he climbed on board and hauled the whole thing across to the new spar tree, riding the donkey all the way across. He thought nothing of this and didn't see what we were so amazed at.

Baker wore the usual logger's uniform, a suit of heavy, green label, Stanfield's underwear with the tattered remnants of a pair of rain-test pants on the lower part and, of course, caulk boots. Walking out along the boom sticks, he followed the normal procedure of using his pike pole as a counterbalance. We were surprised when he told us that he had never learned to swim. Baker was about forty years old and he'd been a farmer in Ontario, with no previous logging experience. When we asked him why he didn't have someone helping him, he said he was too miserable for anyone to live with, and that included women.

While Staff prepared lunch (I remember it was pork chops with all the

trimmings), each of us had a glass of sherry. I asked Bill Baker if he cared to join us. "Sherry, what's that?" he asked. Somebody explained that it was a kind of fortified wine. That was fine with him, he'd try it. But instead of sherry, I got a beer glass and poured in half Hudson's Bay rum and half water, so it came out about the same colour as the sherry. He took it with thanks and dumped about half of it down with the first gulp. Wiping a tear from his eye, he said, "Say, that's not bad stuff," and in a minute he handed his glass back for a refill. I think he had three of these. Then we said our good-byes and he started for shore. That performance was something to see. He was walking on slippery, rolling boomsticks all the way to the beach and at times I swear he was leaning over 45 degrees from the vertical. But he never fell in.

That was Bill Baker. I was sorry to hear about a year later that he died accidentally when a log rolled on him. At least that's what they surmised when they found him a few weeks after.

About an hour after we left Bill, we reached the camp the Americans operated, called Logco. While their official business was going on, I took the dinghy around the point to visit Mr. and Mrs. Jim Stanton. They'd been living in this particular log cabin for thirty-three years of their fifty-two years together. His business was guiding hunters up the river to shoot and/or photograph, grizzly bear. While I was sitting in their cabin talking, a bear got into their cooler on the back porch and Jim simply went out with a broom, swore at the bear, and swatted it. The bear ambled off into the bush.

Next day we left Logco at 11:15 a.m. and arrived back in Vancouver at 8:40 p.m. the day after that. The whole trip had taken less than four days. I was sure that this sort of effi-

ciency would impress my customers and that I would get more charters in the future. But I was mistaken. Tommy explained that in all the years he had been taking them up to Knight Inlet he had taken three days to go up, one day there and three days to come back. They had travelled only a few hours a day, and tied up somewhere and played cards the rest of the time. That was one way they all had a holiday on company time. I never heard from them again.

We call the house at Nelson Island "Potlatch."

My wife, Win, with the produce of our vegetable garden at Nelson Island.

A narrow log bridge connects "Potlatch" to Barbecue Island where, as the name suggests, we have a large barbecue pit. When we bought the place in 1957, the bridge was a single plank wide, with no railing. Many visitors refused to walk the plank, unless well oiled, and had to be taken over by boat. Here I am making the structure a little wider, and safer.

My son Dave, with a wolf eel.

Dick Hawkins, the official totem pole carver at Kingcome Village, carved this pole in honour of King George VI when he came to the throne in 1936.

Dick Hawkins standing in the doorway of a longhouse beside an ancient stone head. This was taken during our first visit in 1956. The stone had been in the possession of the village for as long as anyone can remember. Later, it was stolen from the village and is believed to be somewhere in the US.

Right: Houses in Kingcome Village (Tsawataineuk), 1956. Note the posts under the houses to cope with the Kingcome River in flood.

Another view of the village. The totem is one of the few original poles still standing.

Win with some children around a feast bowl at Kingcome on a later visit in 1963.

The store at Klemtu, an Indian village and cannery on China Hat Island.

SPORTS FISHING WITH DYNAMITE

When it comes to fishing, I prefer dynamite. I say if there is a faster, more efficient way of filling the larder, let's do it.

Herring used to be prolific on the coast. Seine boats caught them by the hundreds of tons in Johnstone Strait and many other areas. They were used mostly for cattle feed and fertilizer. When you wanted a few fresh herring for the table, it was usual to jig for them. A herring jig had about ten tiny barbless hooks on a light line about fifteen feet long with a 10-ounce weight on the bottom end. In most small harbours and bays, if you went out just before sunset, lowered the weight about fifteen feet, and gave it a few jerks, you would pull in the line with a herring wiggling on every hook. Fifteen minutes of this would fill a bucket. Fried herring for breakfast. You could do it anywhere in Pender Harbour, and we regularly did it at Blind Bay, Nelson Island, where we had our cabin.

That was twenty years ago. Then two things happened. First of all, the Japanese market for herring roe opened up. In spawning season, large fleets of seine boats harvested thousands of tons, just for the roe—apparently the Japanese regard it as an aphrodisiac. Over-fishing soon occurred, and the government had to restrict the catch. Second, a new market developed in the United States for bait herring: half-grown herring, frozen, to use as bait for sports fishing. To catch them, fishermen worked at night with brilliant mercury lamps that lit up the whole bay and attracted all the herring to one concentrated spot. There the net would encircle them. One operation in a small place like Ballet Bay and you'd hardly see a herring there again. Some places, like Hidden Basin on Nelson Island, were cleaned right out and the herring have chosen not to return. Even though the slaughter is now somewhat controlled by the government, I do know that you can't jig herring any more in Blind Bay.

When we first had the property at Nelson Island, we availed ourselves of the herring in every way possible—fried, pickled, salted, and smoked. But my friend Bob Gayer and I didn't want to fiddle around with a herring jig. We thought there must be a better way. And there was. I bought a herring gill net, about 100 feet long, which we strung out from the end of our dock towards the next island. After supper we checked the net—and it was gone. Next morning we found it about 200 yards away. A ling cod had come steaming along, right into the centre of the net, tore the whole thing loose and then hung up right at the entrance to the channel. We had 100 feet of net wrapped around one very annoyed ling cod. But not a single herring. Yet we knew they were down there by the thousands. We could see them on the depth sounder like a great black cloud about twelve feet below the surface.

Once again Bob said there must be a better way, and I agreed. I recalled that when we were visiting Thailand, we saw the native fishermen using a circular net, about twenty feet in diameter, attached to a large bamboo ring which they lowered to the bottom of the canal. Once every hour or two, they lifted the ring straight up out of the water on a bridle, which was hoisted to a long bamboo derrick pivoted at the top of a mast. Two or three kids would climb out to the end of the cantilever and their weight lifted the net. I described all this to Bob. He put his mind in gear and he said, "Hell, yes! That will work for us just dandy, but we won't use bamboo or a derrick." Then he described his invention.

He said, "We'll use a plastic tube about three inches in diameter, and about 100 feet long, in the form of a circle with a net stretched between it. We fill the tube with water, sink it to the bottom, wait until there's a good load of unsuspecting fish above it, then open an air valve to the engine room and inflate the tube. It will bounce to the surface with all the fish in the middle, and we'll just have to bail them out."

We convinced ourselves, and anyone else who would listen, that this was indeed the answer. I went to a plastic fabrication outfit in Richmond and had them make up 100 feet of three-inch, bright blue plastic tubing. Then I bought enough net to cover an area of seventy-five square yards. I think the whole bill was about $350, so it had better work.

The next time we were at Nelson Island, we assembled Bob's invention and deployed it alongside our dock in about twenty feet of water. We used four light anchor lines to get it spread out. Then we got the air hose connected to the compressed air whistle tank in the engine room where we had about 100 pounds per square inch pressure. The herring dutifully arrived by the hundreds. Now all we had to do was open the valve—we thought.

I should explain that in twenty feet of water, you need a minimum of ten pounds air pressure to offset this before you can get air into the tube. We had lots of pressure, so no problem. We opened the valve and as soon as five or ten feet of tube inflated, that section immediately rose to the surface dragging one corner of the net with it. Where it promptly burst. It couldn't stand the ten pounds of pressure. By this time the fish were long gone. The sound of hissing air and the sudden appearance of a great writhing blue snake was more than they could stand. We tried every trick we could think of to prevent this from happening, but no way. Nature had us beat.

"I hate to say this," Bob says, "but there is one surefire way, a 'CIL wobbler'—DYNAMITE."

Sounded good to me. It happened that the lime quarry across the bay had closed down, leaving several cases of dynamite behind. We helped ourselves. By experiment, I found that I could fire an electric detonator from a simple six-volt lantern battery. We planned to wrap two sticks of dynamite in waterproof plastic and suspend them on a length of telephone wire twelve feet below a styrofoam float. From there we would take 100 feet of wire across the water to our dinghy, where we had the lantern battery. We waited until after midnight so the local residents could not see what was going on. Even after dark it was easy to locate the position of the large herring school because of the thousands of small bubbles that came to the surface. We quietly paddled out in the dinghy, deployed our bomb, then moved away the required 100 feet with the wire and battery and waited for the herring to come.

"OK, Bob?" I asked. "Just a minute," he said, "let's make sure where it is." Keeping his flashlight low to the water, he searched all around, but he couldn't see the styrofoam float anywhere, until at last we located it— lodged firmly against the side of our dinghy! The telephone wire was coiling up and gently pulling the bomb right underneath us. Bob said, "Christ! We could have had fallen arches."

It was very dark and very quiet. You could hear a pin drop. It took a little fiddling around with anchors before we finally arranged the bomb at a respectful distance. Then, when we heard the herring, I touched the battery terminals and...OOMP! It shook the whole bay and simultaneously lit up the countryside with bright green phosphorescence. I have never seen anything like it. For a few brief mo-

The police launch *Otter* visiting our place at Nelson Island.

ments, you could almost see to read by it. Bright green streaks of fish, probably dogfish, went in every direction.

Dogs started to bark, lights came on, windows and doors opened. We kept absolutely still and waited about half an hour for everyone to go to sleep again. Then we searched around with the flashlight. Everywhere we looked, herring covered the surface, belly up. Bob took a long-handled scoop and began skimming the fish off the water and throwing them into the boat. By the time we collected most of them we were up to our ankles in herring. Enough to last a season, we thought. Back at the dock, we transferred the herring to a large galvanized

wash tub which we filled with water and covered. We would deal with them in the morning.

When morning came, all we found in the tub was hundreds of pairs of eyes and backbones. The herring were immature and had been consumed by their own digestive juices during the night. We now knew why we couldn't catch them in a gill net. They were too small and could swim through the net as if it wasn't there. These were bait herring!

One or two of the neighbours came over and said, "By the way, did you hear what sounded like an explosion last night, about 1 a.m.?" We just shook our heads innocently.

The hippies were a phenomenon that suddenly appeared on the coast in the 1960s and 1970s and they built a lot of these houses. You could always tell a hippie house because at least one of the windows was stained glass. Most of them are abandoned now.

CATCHING PRAWNS

It was not long after getting the place on Nelson Island that we learned it was possible to trap prawns. They are like overgrown shrimp, five or six inches long. But to get them you have to go down deep, about 55 fathoms, 300-350 feet. In those days you couldn't just go down to a hardware store and buy a prawn trap. You built your own.

Our first ones were boxes formed of wooden laths. A trap had an entrance cone at each end and a centre hole about two inches in diameter. The prawns came in through the hole and, if all went well, didn't find their way out. In order to sink this apparatus 55 fathoms, you had to weight it. We usually used two sash weights, one on each lower corner. It was a heavy, clumsy device.

We tried other kinds of traps, but the most successful were made out of large galvanized garbage pails. We simply took the lid off a pail, cut a large hole in it, and installed a galvanized wire funnel. When we put it all together it was heavy enough to sink without added weights, and when we pulled it to the surface, we just unsnapped the lid and dumped out the prawns. I usually carried eight or ten of these traps on board *Blithe Spirit*. Even when they were stacked inside each other, they presented quite a sight. We were jokingly called the "garbage scow": I can remember walking down Cordova Street from the Army and Navy trying to carry six garbage pails, while people looked at me as though I must have a real garbage problem at home.

In those days it was not unusual to get as many as 150 prawns in each trap overnight. However, in the last few years prawn fishing has become an industry, and commercial fishermen now carry as many as a thousand traps on a boat. They have developed a method of laying them one after the other as they proceed at 8 knots. It

doesn't take long to clean most of the prawns out of an area. Nowadays when we put a trap down we are lucky to get five or six overnight.

When we used garbage pails for traps, we laid them out over the bow while we backed up slowly to avoid getting the line in our wheel. First over was a light anchor, about twenty pounds. Then the first trap snapped on the line. We spaced them out roughly ten fathoms apart until we had all ten traps deployed. Then another light anchor, followed by our buoy line, which was about 75 feet with our float and flag on top. But this was too simple to last.

We soon found that the odd inquisitive yachtsman, seeing the flag, would haul up the line to find out what was in the traps. But when they dumped them down again, the cans got jumbled, and when we picked them up the next day they came up in an unholy tangle.

Our first answer to this problem was to make our second anchor about 100 pounds, too heavy for the average yachtsman. We used our electric windlass, but there were other drawbacks. When a tug came along with a boom of logs, he couldn't possibly avoid our flag. So the flag got hung up on the log boom, dragging the rest of the traps behind it. Usually we'd never find them again. We overcame this problem by installing a "break line" so that when the flag got fouled in the log boom, this piece of light line broke. We knew the approximate location of the traps and we used a grapple to find the line and haul them in.

The break line method was too time-consuming, so we developed another plan. We laid the ten traps out in our chosen location and when the last one went down with a light anchor on it, we ran the line to the closest shore, 100–500 feet away. Every 100 feet or so we attached light weights to prevent the line floating

up. When we got to shore, we secured the line around a rock at low tide mark so that it wasn't obvious to passersby. We buried the end and when we went back it was a simple matter, using a drag or even a boat hook, to get the end and recover the traps.

One time we had ten traps laid right out in front of our house in Horseshoe Bay. We could almost see the location from our front windows. Because we were directly in the route of the BC Ferries run to Nanaimo, we needed about 900 feet of line running to the beach. It was excellent prawn fishing at this location, and we had very good luck the first time or two—aside from the fact that sports fishermen, trolling for salmon with deep gear, often hooked our shoreline. We would pick it up festooned with hooks and spoons and flashers. This was all to the good, until one day we went out and there was no hidden anchor and no shoreline. It took many hours of laborious dragging with a grapple hook to get our prawn traps aboard. Some scuba divers who were fishing for ling cod along the beach had come across our bright yellow line. Picking it up, they followed it down to the greatest depth they could go with their diving gear, then cut it off. I have no doubt they found the line very useful.

From all this evolved another tactic. Instead of using a buoy and flag, we tied on an inconspicuous piece of driftwood, no different from hundreds of others floating around on the surface. One day we chose to put our string of traps down at the north end of Bowyer Island in Howe Sound. As usual, we marked it with a piece of driftwood. The next day, we picked up the driftwood, put the line on our windlass, and started hauling in. After we got one or two traps on board, the line began getting heavier and heavier. We were afraid we had hooked under some obstruction. Finally it came to the surface and we found out what

Hauling aboard some traps with the davit and windlass.

had happened.

A commercial prawn fisherman had laid his string of fifty traps right across the top of ours, which of course he didn't know about. Like us, he wanted to avoid predators, so he hadn't marked the position of his traps. When we got his line to the surface, it was so heavy combined with ours that we couldn't pull any more on board. So I cut his line, tied a buoy to one end, and secured the other end to the windlass. Then we hauled in his line with half of his traps. They were the old-fashioned kind made of wood lath and very heavy.

They were all baited with fresh herring. Then we went and picked up the buoy and pulled the rest of his line on board. We thought we should do this because he certainly would never find his traps now that we had dragged them over the bottom of Howe Sound. In the end we had fifty ugly wooden prawn traps piled all over the foredeck, the wheelhouse roof and the boatdeck of *Blithe Spirit*, in addition to our own ten traps. When we arrived back at the West Van Yacht Club, you can imagine the remarks.

None of these commercial traps had any identification. We had no clue

who had put them down. Then someone said they might belong to a prawn fisherman working out of Gibson's Landing. I got on the telephone and eventually ran down Harold Redfern, a man I had known up the coast many years before. He admitted to the ownership of the fifty traps and said that he had been looking all over for them. He came down to the yacht club and loaded them onto his boat. They were still baited with fresh herring, but strangely enough there wasn't a single prawn in any of them. To say that he was annoyed is to put it mildly.

Enjoying the fruits of our labour.

Left: **Blunden Harbour, c. 1975. I remember in the 1930s, about the same time Emily Carr made her famous painting of this scene, I would call in here and find a couple of hundred people.**

The Indian village of Church House. Originally, the government-built village was on the other side of Lewis Channel on Maurelle Island. That place is still called Old Church House, but there's only a bay there now. What the government didn't know until after they built all the houses is that probably the fiercest wind we get on this coast blows down Bute Inlet, and it pretty near levelled the place. So the government moved everything across the channel, about the turn of the century, and that's New Church House. This picture was taken in 1984.

Village Island (Mamalilaculla) in 1989, another deserted Indian village on the coast.

FISH GALORE

Win with her seventy-four pounds of cod.

On one of our northern cruises on *Blithe Spirit*, we were up north of Wells Pass and decided to anchor for the night among the Deserter group of islands at the north end of Queen Charlotte Strait. My friend Bob Gayer was along. Bob loves to fish, but he shares my conviction that results come before sport. They certainly did this time.

When we came out of the harbour next morning, we saw an impressive sight. There must have been 500 excited seagulls circling around something in the water and screaming. They were right over a five-fathom reef. We moved the boat into the middle of the spot and Bob, Win, and I dropped our jiggers overboard. None of us could get a jigger to the bottom before a fish took it. We rapidly began filling the cockpit. There were ling cod, sea bass, rock cod, red snappers, and then a 32-pound halibut! It took both of us with two gaff hooks to get the halibut on board, and when we did he started to object. He managed to flick himself up on edge and then he started thrashing. We all had to evacuate the cockpit. There were three spare 20-pound bottles of propane which he was batting around like billiard balls. He did quite a bit of damage before we managed to subdue him.

Win caught a ling cod that weighed 74 pounds, and then it was Bob's turn. He yelled at me to come and help him. He had a big one coming up. I put my rod down, grabbed the biggest gaff hook on board and reached over the side to see what Bob had. He had hooked a red snapper weighing over thirty pounds. As it came to the surface, its mouth spewed out herring it had just swallowed. Right under this snapper was a huge halibut, following up and swallowing the herring that the snapper was disgorging. I could not believe how big it was. I could only see its head and one fin and this was about five feet across. Ignoring the snapper, I reached down and gaffed the halibut just behind the head. I yelled at Bob to drop his rod and help me, which he did, and we both got on the five-foot gaff handle. The halibut simply ignored us. When he finished swallowing the rest of the herring, he slowly swam away. There was no way we could stop him. He pulled us right back across the cockpit and up against the transom dinghy, then effortlessly pulled the gaff through our hands and swam off. He must have shaken the gaff off because it floated to the surface about 100 feet away. We recovered it after getting Bob's red snapper on board.

What we had encountered was a "herring boil"—millions of herring boiling up over a reef with hundreds of seagulls, ducks and larger fish having a feast. It lasted about two hours, then disappeared. We proceeded down to Alert Bay where we moored at the government floats about 10 p.m. with our cockpit so full of fish we couldn't open the cabin door.

Later, when I told a fisherman about that halibut, he said it probably weighed 150-250 pounds. I asked him how in the world a fisherman could get such a big fish on board. He said they used block and tackle. "But," he added, "you have to pacify them first." When I asked what he meant, he said to use either a .30-.30 or a .303, nothing smaller. As soon as I got to Vancouver, I went to the Army and Navy and bought a .303 Burma rifle which I've carried ever since.

Right: **Bob Gayer carving up the thirty-two-pound halibut, with the rest of our 450 pounds of fish in the background.**

The halibut that didn't get away. In 1990, we caught this eighty-four-pounder off Polkinghorne Island, using a .22 to "pacify" it.

Co-captain and chief engineer of the *Blithe Spirit*, Dudley Meakin, tries a drinking fountain at Tofino. Dudley and I met as fellow radio hams around 1930. He used to own a cabin cruiser with his brother, until his brother went queer and wanted a sailboat. Dudley, like myself, has no time for rag hangers. He and I became joint owners of *Blithe Spirit* instead, and it's the best thing that ever happened. Dudley likes nothing better than to spend most of his waking hours tinkering with it, repairing it, and using it. Today, *Blithe Spirit* has never been in better shape, thanks to Dud. But he doesn't know much about drinking fountains.

Cormorant rookeries in Trincomali Channel.

The author and photographer "on assignment" on Galiano Island in 1975. These sandstone cliffs are a well-known landmark for boaters travelling through Trincomali Channel.

An old steam donkey rusting in the woods in Forward Inlet on the west coast of Vancouver Island. As a young man I used to run one of these machines. Now it is simply a reminder of days gone by.

Index

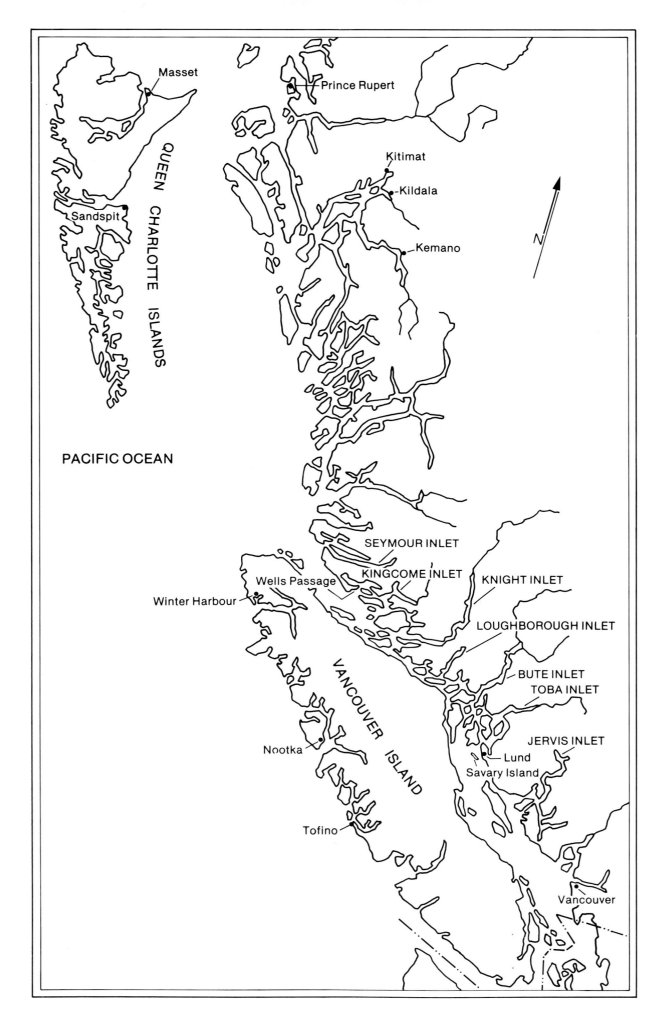

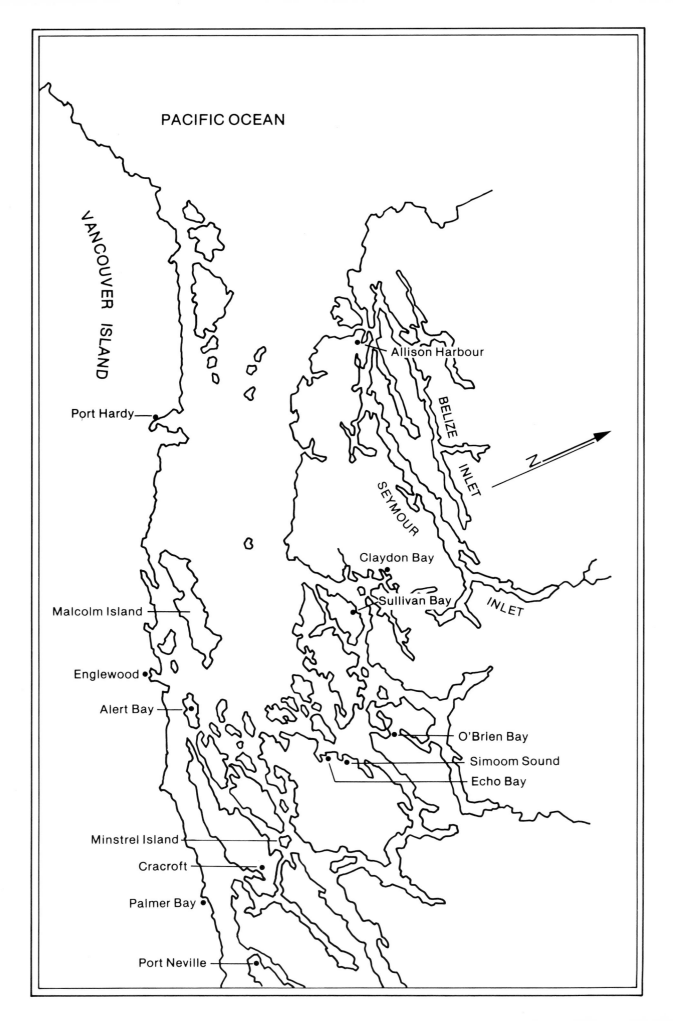